FRED MEIJER - IN HIS OWN WORDS

FRED MEIJER

In His Own Words

INTRODUCTION BY HANK MEIJER

WILLIAM B. EERDMANS PUBLISHING COMPANY
GRAND RAPIDS, MICHIGAN

Copyright © 1995 by Wm. B. Eerdmans Publishing Company
255 Jefferson Ave. S.E., Grand Rapids, Mich. 49503

00 99 98   7 6

Library of Congress Cataloging in Publication Data

Meijer, Fred, 1919-
Fred Meijer, in his own words / introduction by Hank Meijer.
p.   cm.
ISBN 0-8028-7900-4 (pbk.)
1. Meijer, Fred, 1919- . 2. Merchants --Michigan --
Biography. 3. Meijer Inc. -- History. 4. Supermarkets --
Michigan -- History 5. Discount houses (Retail trade) --
Michigan -- History. I. Title.
HF5469.23.U64M4558 1994
381'148'092 --dc20

[B]   94-42705
                                          CIP

To each of the people who wears a Meijer badge,
and to the guests we serve... What a team!

The influence of each human being on others in this life is a kind of immortality.

- JOHN QUINCY ADAMS

Contents

Acknowledgements

This book was planned as a surprise for Fred Meijer, hence any shortcomings reflect upon its editors, not its subject. No doubt it suffers for lack of his knowing participation. That said, it would not have been published without the help of dedicated collaborators.

A team that included Pam Kleibusch, Bill Smith, David Borrink, Armand Aronson, Rob Lang, Bryan Richards and Joe Morello combed archives, sorted photographs and waded through transcripts. Lena Meijer provided further material.

Deborah Meijer, Leslie Stainton and Larry ten Harmsel supplied valuable critiques of the introduction. Merle Struble produced the cover.

Completion of the project depended on David Borrink's design coordination and Larry ten Harmsel's final editing. Sandra DeGroot of Eerdmans saw the manuscript through to publication.

Finally, *In His Own Words* owes its existence to Bill Smith, whose enthusiasm is infectious and judgment astute.

Introduction

His red hair has gone white—but he is still Fred. Only with his sons and grandchildren is it otherwise—"Dad," "Grandpa." To everyone he works with, a corporate family now grown past 60,000, he's "Fred." He's Fred as well to a former president, a couple of governors, congressmen and mayors.

He's just Fred to scores of friends and thousands of customers and wouldn't have it any other way. To his wife he's also Fred—or sometimes "Toots," or "Sunshine," or, with us, in exasperating moments, "*your* father."

He started life more formally, as Frederik Gerhard Hendrik Meijer. The name has a history. It honors both his grandfathers and his father—covering all the bases in the household of Hendrik and Gezina Meijer, where two children were planned and their second, the only son, would be the last.

Frederik Meijer, Fred's paternal grandfather, emigrated from the Netherlands with his son, Hendrik—Fred's father—in 1907. He built ships' boilers at the Stork works, a manufacturing complex in the factory town of Hengelo, near the German border. He drank too much, as did his wife. Holland, Michigan, where he settled in 1907, seemed to help dry him out. He lived to age 80 before he was struck by a car in 1928. Fred has a small boy's memory of Grandpa Meijer as a quiet soul who would send him to the corner store for a tin of Plow Boy tobacco.

Fred was not yet one year old the only time he met his maternal grandfather, Gerhard Mantel. That was in 1920, when Hendrik Meijer, then a barber in Greenville, Michigan, sold his shop, cashed in the family's meager savings, and returned with his wife, Gezina, and their two small children, to Hengelo, where Gezina's mother was dying. Fred's memories of Grandpa Mantel were thus more remote—although made the more vivid by the aura which surrounded the Mantel clan. Where the Meijers were factory folk given to drink, the puritanical Mantels had loftier ambitions. They belonged to a network of Dutch radicals: socialists and anarchists, in an era before the Russian Revolution when the two could coexist. They were engaged in what sometimes seemed like every political, cultural and economic conflict of their day.

His employers regarded Gerhard Mantel as a troublemaker. He was fired from his job in the Stork mill for reasons not quite clear in Fred's memory, but having something to do with protests on behalf of renters who were denied the right to vote. Unhealthy working conditions were also a cause for complaint. (Tuberculosis was often a condition of retirement.) In either case, Mantel became a shoemaker, then a tailor. With the degree of independence a trade afforded him, he could spend the rest of his life engaged in the crusades that would animate some of his children as well, including Gezina right up to her death in 1978.

Mantel fought the government, the capitalists (largely interchangeable in his eyes), the church, overpopulation, and later Nazi occupation. He and his wife espoused birth control, women's rights, pacifism, vegetarianism, varieties of left-wing politics. It was a radical's stew of the free-thinking and the puritanical that would color the life of a boy named Fred.

Back in Greenville, in that farmhouse on the north edge of town where Fred was born on December 7, 1919, he was known less often by his name than by his position in the family. Back then, in a nuclear household of two parents, a daughter, and a son, he was known simply as "Brother." His older sister, Johanna, was born in 1916, four years after Hendrik and Gezina settled in Greenville. They were "Sister" and "Brother," and so it would remain until well after the doors opened in 1934 on a little grocery store on Lafayette Street.

Fred took after his mother physically, but her austere and earnest ways were tempered in the boy by the restless expansiveness of his father. For five years Hendrik had worked at a half dozen trades, traveling the country, before going to barber school in Chicago. In 1912 he landed in Greenville as a rookie barber, given a chance to prove himself in a temporary job. He liked the job and the town. Only then did Gezina join him. A family followed, and a degree of prosperity as well. Had the prosperity held, Fred might have gone to college—perhaps to become a history teacher.

But that's getting ahead of our story, which is the tale of the boy who skinny-dipped in the cool waters of the Flat River and made watercress sandwiches from plants on the banks of Edwards Creek. He was a buck-toothed boy, shy around girls, earnest about his schoolwork, a maverick only in his heart.

At his birth his mother nursed him in tandem with the neighbor woman's baby. The only flowers Gezina received to mark the event came from Ellis Ranney, the refrigerator tycoon who was one of Hendrik's most faithful patrons.

Fred's academic record at Pearl Street School and Greenville High was forever overshadowed by his more scholarly sister. Yet the December baby was sufficiently precocious to be advanced to classes with his peers born earlier in the year. He took up the clarinet and the violin. At play, if he wasn't building tunnels in the farmyard or riding his pony, Fred was keeping meticulous records about his calf for the 4-H Club.

Brother and Sister helped out with their father's struggling dairy business. Hendrik dreamed of turning from barber to dairy farmer, among other things. He named his venture the Model Dairy, after the showplace enterprise in Chicago owned by utility magnate Samuel Insull. This Model Dairy never quite lived up to its name, however. Fred delivered milk after school with a horse and wagon. Gezina milked the cows and labored over the bottle washer. Hendrik could never afford to give up his barber's income. Pasteurizing equipment, perhaps the Model Dairy's only hope, was beyond reach. And as the effects of the stock market crash of 1929 sank in, what had been a struggling business became a dying one.

The Great Depression was a defining event of Fred's youth, indeed of his generation. It turned his life and millions of others' in less certain directions. The remarkable thing was that from the devastation bloomed such a store as came to be.

Hendrik had always been restless. Never planning to remain a barber, he had tried selling furnaces, peddling lace, nearly opening a furniture store, raising chickens, and, most seriously, running a dairy.

The onset of bad times hit barbers hard. Haircuts quickly became luxuries many could do without. Hendrik had not anticipated this when he built the three storefronts above his basement barbershop. He told the banker who approved the mortgage that he would rent out the storefronts. He told his thrifty wife the rent would provide them with income in their later years. He found two tenants readily enough. He tried and tried and never found another. No income meant no mortgage payment. In another day, foreclosure would have been inevitable. But this was the Depression. What did the bank want with yet another near-worthless building? Better to keep the mortgage-holder, who was an honorable man, on the hook in hopes of someday realizing something.

Hendrik had tried to interest a grocery chain in his space: A&P, Kroger both said no. Then a wholesale grocery in Grand Rapids, itself hungry for business, told Hendrik that if he had an acceptable credit reference, he could be set up in business for himself. This was not what Hendrik had in mind. But by 1934, as he approached his 50th birthday, he was ready once more for the strange turns with which fate confronts us.

Fred was 14 years old when his father decided to open the little North Side Grocery near the corner of Lafayette and Charles. The teenager nailed up used wooden lath to prepare the walls of the unfinished storefront for plastering. He watched his father barter a violin to the plasterer who finished the job.

The little store had a counter to the left of the doorway, with an old cash register, coffee mill and scales, as "Sister"—Johanna— remembers it. Beside the counter a stand held account pads for each of the store's charge customers. In back was a refrigerated case for milk, cheese and butter. Hendrik kept working part-time in his old barbershop even after he'd sold it to his assistant to raise the money to outfit the store. Johanna had just graduated from Greenville High School, where she was valedictorian. Although she dreamed of college, she would spend a year running the new store. Fred worked every spare minute as well, nights and weekends. The rituals of high school—football games, dances, the soda fountain—were not to be his.

In another time and place he might have been in the second generation of his family's business. Or, as he insists, he might have taught history. Instead, in his career, the generations blurred. The times forced his to go to work, but there was more to it than that. He also shared the entrepreneurial zeal and founder's instincts of his father, and then grafted onto those traits essentials of managing a continuing business: the steady hand, the willingness to delegate authority and share credit. And he thrived on every minute of it.

By the time Fred graduated from Greenville High in 1937, the little store had taken on new possibilities. It had survived, first of all, against the competition of A&P and Kroger and nearly a score of other small grocery outlets in Greenville.

The business was changing rapidly. The old pads for charge accounts, as well as the filling of a customer's order—chiefly by Johanna or Fred from stock behind the counter—gave way to cash sales in 1936 and self-service in 1937. The store expanded to accommodate such change. It was poised—as were how many others, including the chain stores—on the eve of the Supermarket Age.

Offering value appealed to Hendrik and Fred. Low prices were in their bones. Their work showed promise. They began to think, in this era of chains, about a second store. Johanna had earned a scholarship to the University of Michigan. Two years later, Fred might have followed suit. He was tempted, and torn. The money would have been hard to come by, but somehow the family would have scraped it together. Yet he felt more strongly the tug—literally, in this instance—of a grocer's apron strings.

With war in Europe and a draft looming, Fred tried to enlist in the army. Then, as later, when summoned by the Selective Service, the hernia that would someday require surgery sent him packing back to Greenville.

On December 7, 1941, Fred was celebrating his twenty-second birthday. He lay on the rug in the sunny front room listening to music when the sensational news of a Japanese surprise attack came over the radio. Again he made the trips to Detroit, again the armed forces turned him down.

He had hoped to fulfill his service and get on with his career. The store that challenged the A&P had become a thriving enterprise, expanded into a supermarket with baskets on wheels which customers pushed to help themselves. It boasted the longest meat counter in the county. Its low prices and friendly service had built a following. And the way the family responded to the Depression's dramatic legacy—treating the customer with a welfare order just the same as the customer in the shiny new Packard—brought what was now the Meijer's Thrift Super Market 60 per cent of the relief orders in Montcalm County. It was a staggering figure for one store among two dozen competitors.

From as early as Fred could remember, his father involved him not only in the labor of whatever project he had embarked upon, but in the decisions relating to that project as well. If he was trading a horse or buying a cow or talking over a loan with a banker, he brought Fred along. When a salesman came into the original grocery store and Hendrik was next door in the barbershop, the children were in charge. As with Johanna before him, young Fred had been trusted to deal with the bread man or the wholesaler's truck driver. Indeed, even when Hendrik and Fred were together, Hendrik might nudge Fred ahead and let him do the talking. It was a seamless relationship. The trust was implicit and complete.

Together they attended in 1940 their first meeting of a fledgling trade association, the Supermarket Institute. Here was Fred at 20 years old, conferring with men old enough to be his father or grandfather, entrepreneurs building great chains of new stores. Here was Hendrik, in his late 50s, conscious of his heavy Dutch accent, inspired to pursue what would have been a hollow adventure without his son at his side. They came back from that meeting in Kansas City seeing no reason, once the question of Fred's military status was resolved, why they too could not build a chain of stores.

They had long had they been driving on Sunday afternoons to other towns around the county and beyond. They weighed the competition, the availability of real estate. Soon after Pearl Harbor, they settled on a vacant Chevy garage in the town of Cedar Springs, 15 miles north of Grand Rapids.

It was wartime, then, as they set about remodeling the building. Johanna would soon be drafted by the family to run that store, while Fred spent most of his time in Greenville. (Among the first generation of cashiers hired to work in the Greenville store was a farm girl Fred's age from a German Lutheran settlement near Lakeview. Her name was Lena Rader. She would remember that Cedar Springs grand opening, her first, and the Pillsbury salesman who played over and over on the scratchy phonograph the only song he had, the "Wabash Cannonball.")

Now, with two stores, they were a chain. Fred's ambitions, purged of college, concentrated upon the business. Their scope was limited then only by the breadth of his vision—and the constraints of war. In a business necessarily obsessed with detail, the notion of growth satisfied larger needs. It became its own engine of excitement. A second store, for Fred, could only be a prelude to a third.

In the meantime, however, there were ration cards—limits on gasoline for the car and truck, limited supplies of metals for store fixtures, shortages of everything from jelly to pork. As they had danced with the tax collector over Depression-era novelties such as social security, now Fred and his father tangoed through a maze of wartime regulation and scarcity.

In 1946 the ceiling began to lift. Soon after the end of the war came Fred's January marriage to Lena Rader in the farmhouse where she had been born. Their honeymoon took them to New Orleans, with stops at other grocery stores en route. In Cincinnati they visited with William Albers, formerly the president of the Kroger Company, who had gone out on his own with a chain of supermarkets.

Later that year, Johanna married Don Magoon, a scholarly Army captain returning from occupied Japan. They too settled in Greenville. In the meantime, the family had set about opening its third store, in the county seat town of Ionia, between Grand Rapids and Lansing.

That building was just weeks away from opening the night the siren sounded atop the fire barn in Greenville and Fred and Lena heard a tapping on their bedroom window. A fireman had come to rouse them: the store was on fire. They lived only half a mile away, but by the time they raced down Lafayette Street the old building with its nine additions, its big meat counter, its invoices still on nails in the backroom office—was consumed in smoke and flame. Fred managed to dart in the smoky rear entrance and save a few papers and ledgers. That was it.

The next day, alerted to the availability of a war-surplus quonset hut in a town to the north, the family ordered it delivered to a site they already owned nearly across the street from the smoldering ruins of the original store. Temporarily they set up a produce stand there—this was July—and within weeks they were back in business. It was a struggle, with the cash flow burden of a soon-to-open store in Ionia now increased dramatically by the cost of replacing an underinsured building and an uninsured inventory. (And with rationing just ended, a small treasure of hard-to-get beef had also been ruined.) The next month the Ionia store opened. The chain had grown to three.

Fred and Lena did not start a family as quickly as they expected. Instead, Lena continued to work in the business—in the office, where she fought back tears wrestling to overhaul a dismal bookkeeping set-up until auditors from Grand Rapids came in and began to turn it into a system. Lena then turned to advertising layout. Fred was absorbed in the endless detail of the business. With Hendrik he traveled from store to store. If he took time for Rotary, or to stop for pie on the road between towns, it was usually Hendrik's idea. Fred never drank coffee.

In 1949 the company opened its first stores in Grand Rapids, the largest city in the region. It was here that Hendrik and Fred had come from the first, to buy on the produce market, to visit the wholesaler, to study the newest big city supermarkets. It was here that the brokers and salesmen were based. It was here too that more customers, more opportunities awaited than in all the small towns combined. Fred and Don Magoon determined to relocate the company's office to Grand Rapids, and they did so in 1952 with the opening of the company's third Grand Rapids supermarket on the northeast side. The store opened the week Lena went into the hospital for the birth of their first of three sons. With the doctor's summons to a Cesarean section tears fell onto the layout sheet as she tried to finish an ad at a card table in the living room.

The corporate office was located on the second floor at the back of the store. Fred shared his with his father, and they could look through a window down at the long grocery aisles. They knew everyone who worked in the stores. The company picnics were family affairs. When some of the clerks approached them in 1951 about starting an independent union, they were sympathetic.

In the next five years, Lena and Fred had two more sons. They moved from a modest two-story to a larger contemporary house designed by a cousin and built alongside a golf course. Both parents were active in the PTA, manning booths at school carnivals and filling their succession of station wagons for school field trips.

It was in the 1950s that the supermarket consolidated its claim to symbolizing the American dream. Here was gleaming abundance. Here was technology come home, from electric-eye doors to frozen foods to mammoth computers. The company doubled in size in the next half dozen years. It improved its buying by joining a national cooperative which supplied products under the Food Club label—forerunners of Meijer-label grocery products. It improved its distribution by creating its own warehouse. Fred shared these challenges with his father and his brother-in-law, but the vigor with which they were pursued reflected his energy. It was at his urging as well that the company began offering trading stamps, and then, recognizing stamps as an impediment to offering lower prices, it was Fred who reversed field in 1960 and took the company off stamps.

Fred, Hendrik and Don Magoon and their families all lived on the same block on the northeast side of Grand Rapids. Fred looked up to his brother-in-law, listened to and respected his opinions on a variety of issues, yet operated as well with an innate confidence born of the trust and experience that came from two decades of sharing decisions almost daily with his father.

In 1959 the company entered into merger negotiations with Plumb Supermarkets, a strong chain in the Muskegon area with whom Meijer hoped to have some synergy. Although the merger fell through, the way it would have changed what had been parallel roles and ownership for Fred and Don brought Don's long-standing frustrations to the surface and opened a rift which would last for decades.

Later in 1960 Don and Johanna Magoon left the company. In bitter negotiations that followed, Fred, against the advice of his father, agreed to buy Don and Johanna's share of the company for a price that was nearly as much as the total book value of the enterprise. The parting left a bitter split between father and daughter. Don became a consultant, and also tested a new concept in telephone shopping that anticipated some of the innovations currently coming into vogue. He ultimately accepted an appointment as professor of business at Eastern Michigan University.

It was a difficult period for Fred as well, but perhaps a necessary prelude to the innovation he would soon become involved in—the experiment which altered the destiny of a little grocery chain in western Michigan.

By 1960 the country was already seeing the proliferation of a retail format known as the discount store. These were upstart mass retailers with little style or sophistication. Their raison d'etre was defiance of the fair trade laws which allowed manufacturers to set the price for their product, and by which traditional department and specialty stores abided. The discounters flouted these rules, piled products high and sold them cheap—not unlike the early supermarkets. It was their ability to live with narrower profit margins which distinguished them from their competitors.

Supermarkets and discount stores began to locate side by side. Here and there a supermarket operator tried to create his own discount store. The experiments were not lost on Fred and his father.

In 1961 they failed, rather as Hendrik had with the storefront next to his barbershop almost thirty years earlier, to find a discount store operator they could lease space to. In this case the space was an 80,000-square foot addition to a supermarket on the southeast side of Grand Rapids. Here again, in a broad-brush way, history would repeat itself.

Fred and Hendrik discovered that to be a discounter required a good bit of risk—but relatively little merchandising skill so long as most of the sales space was leased out to people who knew what they were doing. Meijer could become, in effect, the glorified landlord for an agglomeration of tenants under one roof. So they set about signing leases and designing a store that would combine their supermarket with a discount house.

They were well along with their planning—undeterred by a consultant who counseled otherwise—when they arrived back at the Fuller Street office one day. Hendrik grew quiet as Fred weighed aloud the gamble they were about to undertake. "Well," Fred asked his father, "do you think we should do it?"

At first his father did not answer. Then he said, "No."

Fred was taken aback. "I knew he was in favor of it," he recalled. "Why not?" Fred asked.

"Because I'm too old to see it through. If we go broke in this deal, I don't want you to tell yourself, 'I did it because my dad wanted it.'" Thus gradually had the torch been passed.

Construction was already underway when the months of research and reflection led to another turning point. Fred and Hendrik and their colleagues abandoned the expected approach of using two sets of cash registers, one for a supermarket side, the other for the discount store. Instead, not only would all the departments be under one roof, they would also share a single bank of registers—this was true one-stop shopping.

Even as that decision was made, the company committed itself to the combination-store concept in a way that today seems almost foolhardy. Ground was broken for addition to the Holland super-market and for a completely new building in Muskegon. The Grand Rapids store opened in June, and that fall brought the next two. With a suddenness that could have destroyed the little super-market chain, the company now had three Thrifty Acres stores in operation, and costs piling up faster than the money in the cash registers.

Fred and Hendrik may have been glorified landlords, but those three stores held more retail space than the rest of their supermar-kets combined. Cash flow couldn't keep up with expenses. Long-time Meijer executive Harvey Lemmen recalled the day when they were so far behind on their obligations that Fred came into his office "white as a sheet." But the glorified landlords proved to be quick studies. The bought out leases of troubled tenants, learned to negotiate on Seventh Avenue, and tried every which way to attract customers to their new form of shopping. Slowly prospects bright-ened.

In 1964, with two more big stores under construction, Hendrik died. Fred lost the partner he had worked with so intimately for 30 years. He accepted a new role, and helped his mother accept a new one too. She became president, then chairman and chairman emerita.

Dad was keenly interested in his family. He tried to juggle demands of business with life at home, and frequently the two overlapped. Lena was a pillar of patience. Together, with the boys in the back of the station wagon, they constantly visited stores—religiously, I'm tempted to say, since it was very nearly ritual to spend a Sunday driving to Kalamazoo or Muskegon. (The old Kalamazoo stores had vending machines for food service. We could each pick out a sandwich from behind the machine's little windows.) We would pester Mom in the toy department while Fred consulted with the store manager and said hello to as many associates as he could.

Car trips also took us to more distant points—to Washington or Florida or the Wisconsin Dells, to Tahquamenon Falls or Boston. We absorbed the roll of the country, fought for the rollaway bed in small motels, wrestled in the back of the station wagon. Dad, it should be noted, toured stores along the way. He was diligent at home as well. He built a treehouse in the backyard that overlooked a fairway of the golf course. When we took up skiing, he installed bindings in his basement workroom.

As the company grew in size, his stature as a civic leader grew. He led a campaign for an urban renewal project in downtown Grand Rapids. He was committed to an integrated society, pioneering the hiring and inclusion of African-Americans in Grand Rapids. He played a prominent role in the Urban League.

In the late 1960s, he became an early critic of American involvement in the war in Vietnam. It was an outspoken position for a merchant whose livelihood depended on an appeal to a great mass of customers. But it was also consistent with the way he was raised. Gezina, still active in the company and visiting stores as religiously as Fred, certainly approved.

Nor was it surprising that he would identify with early campaigns for environmental awareness—nor that such a tendency would reveal itself more spectacularly today.

While the company was profitable, Fred rarely took a dividend. He and Lena have always lived modestly. They remain in the same comfortable house they built in 1957. Fred recently bought a new car after years of using high-mileage ones that had been driven by other Meijer executives. His preferred vacations have been bicycle trips, walking tours or educational travel, his choice of lodging usually a budget motel.

Fred's frugality as an individual stands in direct contrast to his willingness to commit all resources to building a healthy company. His suits are inexpensive—and ideally off the rack at Meijer—but the building where those suits (and shirts and shoes and watches) are sold is state of the art. The need to control costs is dictated by the demands of a competitive environment, not by the needs of a spendthrift owner.

That the company remains healthy is testament to lessons learned since those first turbulent days of Thrifty Acres. Bouts of overexpansion forced on Fred and his colleagues the discipline of bank ratios. The accounting systems Lena lacked and Don Magoon began evolved into ever more precise measures.

Yet if by the 1980s the company began to grow in a more consistent pattern, experimentation never stopped. One retail analyst reported in 1994 that Fred's company had failed at every one of its diversification efforts since the big one in 1962. True in a way, yet ultimately a misreading of the dynamics of the company Fred built.

Meijer's men's and women's specialty stores, called "Copper Rivet," "Tansy" and "Sagebrush," flourished when brands such as Levi's held young America in thrall and were not available to discount stores. When the magic of certain brands faded, these stores did too, and they were sold. The shift from supermarkets to what we know today as supercenters meant Meijer had some old buildings to recycle. Two of these formed the basis of what might have been a chain of discount drug stores. The Meijer experiment (called "Spaar") quickly built sales, but to reach a critical mass of stores would have required diverting attention as well as money from the big stores, and the big stores were just plain more exciting.

The company's acquisition of a group of discount stores in Ohio at the height of Michigan's recession again confirmed the superiority of the big stores, and these old-line discount stores were either expanded or sold off. More recently, in 1992, the company began opening membership wholesale clubs, only to close these the next year. In hindsight, it had entered too late a niche which had not expanded as expected—indeed, a niche that was beginning to consolidate between the time the company committed to the experiment and the time the first club opened.

Within Meijer, however, these bids at diversity are not looked upon as failures. They are the necessary by-product of that very restlessness and receptiveness that drove Hendrik to open the first store and Fred to forge ahead with the big stores. The stores themselves reflect that creativity, with myriad refinements of the concept of one-stop shopping. If Fred has been obsessed with details—with toilet doors that open out, for example—he has also been obsessed with the need to change.

Time forces change, of course. Gezina died in 1978. Fred's sons graduated from college, and two of three came to work in the business, while the third is an active member of the board of directors. Lena's long resume now includes a seat on the board as well.

The company grew from three big stores to five to dozens, from the Grand Rapids area to Michigan, Ohio and Indiana, Illinois and Kentucky. The company's warehousing expanded to Lansing, southeastern Michigan and southwestern Ohio. Fred's office moved from the old supermarket to a modern facility, dubbed not immodestly the "Fred Meijer Building."

With the elevation of long-time Grand Rapids Congressman Gerald R. Ford to the presidency, Fred became involved in a local effort to create the Gerald R. Ford Presidential Museum. The conference room next to his office is adorned with the the mementoes of that undertaking.

Over the years, Fred and the company have participated in nearly every civic initiative of consequence in Grand Rapids. For the first time in the 1990s, however, Fred sought to put his own stamp on a venture that, like so much of the company's early growth, would not have succeeded without his active involvement.

He quietly began amassing the largest collection of major works by renowned sculptor Marshall Fredericks when he was approached by the president of the local horticultural society with a proposition that Meijer support the creation of a botanic garden. The timing was right. The sculptures were a collection in search of a home. The ultimate site for the garden was property Meijer owned on the northeast side of Grand Rapids.

The project held a special resonance for Fred. It could be home to the sculptures, it could be a laboratory and classroom for that environmental awareness that strikes Fred as so central to man's place on the earth, and it could reflect Lena's love of flowers and plants.

Thus was born the Frederik Meijer Gardens. The main greenhouse structure is the Lena Meijer Conservatory. The work of Fredericks and other sculptors will grace the grounds. One of the works is in a real sense Fred's conception: a bronze pine stump cast from one of the stumps Lena's father cleared from his 40-acre farm in Montcalm County at the turn of the century. The idea, which was solely his and which weathered the laughter of friends and family, resulted in the permanent preservation of what might be considered a Michigan icon, the last vestige of an era that forever changed a wilderness landscape.

Fred has expressed his enthusiasm for the environment in other ways as well. He helped preserve a pristine lake in northern Kent County, and became, quite inadvertently, the most generous donor anywhere to the national Rails-to-Trails project by underwriting the acquisition of abandoned railroad right-of-way for a 29-mile bicycle path in Montcalm County that starts not far from the farm where he was born.

While civic works are the happy by-product of a frugal entrepreneur's generosity, it is within the company he helped create that Fred finds his greatest satisfaction. Talent has flourished. Reserved parking spaces are unthinkable. His colleagues are his friends—

rarely socially, for he prefers a quiet night at home, reading—but in the sense of comrades in a career-long adventure.

An Irish supermarket operator said recently that he always remembered Fred's answer when he asked him several years ago what his most important job was at Meijer. Fred thought for a moment and said, "I guess I help set the tone."

Words and phrases like "sensitivity" and "corporate culture" belong to the language of our age. If there is one word dearest to Fred, it is "dignity." A sense of the dignity of each human being—and the respect to which we are entitled by virtue of our humanity—is at the core of his belief.

He walks briskly with a double mission: to work with people and to solve problems. In his world the second cannot be accomplished without the first, and the first cannot be contemplated without an appreciation of the thoughts and opinions of others. It was what he grew up watching his father do. It is what he has tried to help his sons understand. It is the "tone" he tries to set that has to inform the careers of the people he works with if the company is to be successful in the broadest meaning of success. And it is a direct reflection of a Dutch homily he learned from his father and keeps on a plaque in his office: "Niet ik, niet jij, maar wij." ("Not I, not you, but we.")

Fred Meijer embodies the contradictions of his life—and of a Dutch heritage of peaceableness and schism. He is the puritan with a rebel's disdain for convention. He combines an obsession with safety, sanitation, even security with a delight in risk and adventure. He is a bundle of opinions and a seeker of consensus. But this book is not about Fred—it *is* Fred. In his own words.

—HANK MEIJER
GRAND RAPIDS, 1995

Chronology

1919 Fred Meijer born in Greenville, Michigan

1920 Prohibition becomes law; women's suffrage amendment
1923 Hendrik Meijer constructs building in Greenville for his
      barbershop and other tenants
1927 Babe Ruth hits 60 home runs
1928 Hendrik builds storefronts next to barbershop for
      rental property
1929 Stock market crash

1933 Adolf Hitler named German chancellor
1934 Hendrik and family open grocery store in vacant
      storefront; Johanna graduates from high school
1935 Social Security becomes law; "Thrift Market" switches from credit
      sales to "strictly cash,"
1936 Thrift Market goes self-service
1937 Fred graduates from high school; Thrift Market doubles
      in size
1938 Orson Welles shocks nation with "War of the Worlds"
1939 German troops invade Poland

1940 Fred and Hendrik attend their first meeting of Super
      Market Institute; store expands again, now a "supermarket"
1941 Lena Rader hired as cashier; Japanese planes attack Pearl Harbor
1942 Cedar Springs store opens, to be managed by Johanna
1945 World War II ends; atomic bombs begin nuclear age
1946 Fred marries Lena Rader; Johanna marries Don Magoon;
      original Greenville store burns; Ionia store opens
1947 Jackie Robinson first black to play major league baseball
1949 First Meijer supermarket opens in Grand Rapids

1950 Korean War begins
1951 Consolidated Independent Union organized
1952 Company offices move to Grand Rapids above new Store #6 on
      northeast side; son Hank born
1954 Son Doug born

1957 *Son Mark born; Federal troops integrate Little Rock schools;*
      Elvis appears on Ed Sullivan Show
1958 *U.S. launches first satellite*

1960 *Proposed merger with Plumb collapses; Johanna and Don Magoon*
      leave company; premium stamp program dropped in favor of
      lower prices
1962 *"Thrifty Acres" stores open in Grand Rapids, Muskegon*
      and Holland; Cuban missile crisis
1963 *President Kennedy assassinated*
1964 *Hendrik Meijer dies at age 80*
1966 *First Lansing store opens, #23*
1968 *Martin Luther King, Robert Kennedy assassinated*
1969 *First Meijer gas stations open; Meijer stores open Sundays;*
      First man on moon

1973 *OPEC quadruples price of oil*
1974 *First Detroit-area store opens, #32; Lansing distribution center*
      opens; Nixon resigns; Gerald Ford becomes president
1975 *Vietnam War ends with fall of Saigon*
1978 *Gezina Meijer dies at age 91*
1979 *Meijer acquires Jean House specialty store chain*

1980 *Spaar discount drugstores open*
1981 *Twin Fair stores acquired in Ohio*
1982 *Fred receives honorary Doctor of Humanities from Grand Valley*
      State University
1984 *New Meijer logo adopted*
1985 *Fred wins Food Marketing Institute Sidney R. Rabb Award;*
      new office, #985, opens
1986 *Space shuttle Challenger explodes*
1988 *Meijer stores open 24 hours*
1989 *Berlin Wall crumbles*

1990 *Last Meijer supermarket, #6, closes*
1991 *Iraq routed in Gulf War*
1992 *SourceClub opens (closes in 1993); riots hit Los Angeles*
1993 *Meijer begins accepting charge cards for groceries*
1994 *First Indiana stores open, #120, 121; ground broken for first Illinois*
      store; seven-week strike in Toledo; baseball strike cancels World Series
      for first time in 90 years; American troops occupy Haiti
1995 *Frederik Meijer Gardens open; Meijer opens first store in Illinois:*
      #146 in Champaign

CHAPTER 1

~

THE 20s

TROUBLE AT BIRTH

My dad had a problem when I was born: the doctor wouldn't come. They had arranged with Dr. Bracey to tend to my mother when I was born, and Dr. Bracey got sick. So they tried to get another doctor, and called a Dr. John R. Hanson. When Dr. Hanson found out it was a rush call, and it was Henry Meijer, he said no way was he coming. My dad said how come? He says, you haven't paid me for the last baby. And my dad says, you didn't tend to my wife on the last baby. He says, I did and you didn't pay me. And my dad says, you did not, and I did pay the doctor, and I didn't pay you and you didn't tend to my wife when our daughter was born. They had quite a discussion over that, until the doctor said, you're Henry Meijer the barber. Oh, I'm so sorry, Henry. I'm talking about a different Henry Meyer that has a whole slug of kids and didn't pay me for the last baby. I'm sorry. I'll be right out, Henry. And he was right over. So you see, I had all kinds of problems getting born.

HALF A HAIRCUT

I can remember going down to the barbershop and cutting up newspapers for my dad's shaving papers. We cut them into pieces about 10" square and made a stack of them and those were the papers he would wipe his razor on. I remember getting my hair cut in the barbershop and how if a customer came in, my dad would send us to school with half a haircut. Actually it looked okay. It wasn't cut half on one side, he just hadn't finished it, but we felt so self-conscious going to school without a complete haircut.

I was (still am) a bashful kid whose parents brought out my best

*Fred (left) and
sister Johanna in
Greenville, 1920*

*Below: Hendrik
in his first
barbershop,
Greenville, 1912*

NO FUTURE

Dad always figured he never got a promotion in the Netherlands because he was home reading a socialist newspaper one day when the company man came and visited my Grandpa when he was ill, and that probably went on the record someplace. From that time on he could never get a promotion. Maybe that wasn't the reason at all. Maybe it was just my Dad's imagination. He always felt the employers also had an agreement that if you were a good worker, they didn't want you moving from one place to another so you couldn't get hired away.

SACRIFICE REMEMBERED

My mother and dad worked very hard together. They had a very good life. They respected each other, and they were friends as well as being husband and wife, and it might sound like an odd thing to say, but I think mutual respect is terribly important for any relationship. My mother was so grateful that my father would spend all their family savings so she could go back to see her mother in the Netherlands when she was dying. She told me about that time and time again. My dad could have done nothing more to show his compassion or love or being a good husband to her than to take all their money and go back to see her mother. That one demonstration of love just impressed her. How few men, after they have been in the United States from 1907 until 1920, as my dad had been, would have spent all their earnings and come back to the United States and start over again so his wife could go home and see her mother--she really appreciated that.

I credit my Parents who gave me my feeling of Self worth.

Fred (below left), age three, stands with his father outside the building Hendrik began in 1923. Hendrik moved his barbershop into the basement and later built the storefronts to the right (above) which housed the first Meijer grocery store. For a time during the Depression, the family lived in the corner building's second-story apartment

SPITTING ON THE GRIDDLE

I can remember the kerosene lantern days when we would do the work in the barn in the dark winter evenings. We didn't have electricity in the barn, and we'd walk there with a kerosene lantern. In the early store, we pumped kerosene for people who would buy it by the gallon or 5 gallons and take it home and burn their kerosene lanterns or their kerosene stoves. We used to have a kerosene stove in the back room of our home where it was an alternate to the kitchen stove that wasn't fired up in the summertime.

I remember having my aunt and uncle over for dinner, my Aunt Ann from Holland, Michigan, I think it was, and my mother asked me to see if the griddle was hot. She used to just spit a little bit on her iron to see if it was hot enough, so I went into the kitchen and then came out and said,"I just spit on the griddle, and it's warm enough." I suppose it was purified by boiling, but it isn't a very good thing to spit on the griddle where you're going to make the pancakes. I think my mother told me that quite quickly.

THE DITCH

I was digging a ditch in the barnyard with the neighbor boys. My mother says to my dad, "You can't have that ditch in the barnyard."

My dad always took the kids' point of view and he said, "Don't worry about it." What we did was put old boards over it and then we put carpeting over it, then we put sand over it. You could hardly see the thing. Then we'd crawl through that ditch and under the chicken coop wall. The chicken coop didn't have a cement wall so we could dig right under and then we'd sit in the chicken coop. That was our clubhouse.

So, my mother said, "Well, you can't have that, the cows will step it in."

My dad said, "Don't worry about it. They'll dig it out and then we'll have them fill it up again." Now, I can't remember filling it up. I have a feeling that I went out and my dad said, "Let's fill it up." Then he filled 90 percent and I filled 10 percent. I don't remember filling it, I remember digging it. But we had a ball.

The family's short-lived prosperity during the 1920s is evident in this portrait of Gezina, Johanna, Hendrik and Fred

HARD WORK

My sister was a very dynamic lady and always enjoyed giving her younger brother orders. I figure that's the prerogative of an older sister so it didn't bother me. She worked very hard. The whole family worked very hard. We were all needed. If I didn't come into the store right after school, we'd have to hire someone at 20 cents an hour or whatever we paid them. If that's four hours or five hours, that's 80 cents or one dollar.

I never bought a Coca-Cola the entire time I was in high school, and I always handled family money. On the milk route I was handling it from the time I was eight years old until we got rid of the milk route, when we went into the grocery business and sold the milk in the store.

No one even thought of an allowance. As we grew older if we needed some books or something, we'd talk it over. When we were in the milk business we got up to 200 quarts a day. We started out in 1929 at 12 cents a quart, ended up in the depths of the Depression at a nickel a quart. When we went into the grocery business, we sold milk in the store at two quarts for 15 cents. Let's say the peak is 200 quarts a day and the milk, let's say, was 8 cents a quart. I don't know whether it was 6 or 10 or whatever it was. It certainly wasn't 10 when we did 200 quarts a day. But, if it was 8 cents a quart a day and the highest we ever got was 200 quarts, the highest we ever took in was $16 a day.

CHURCH

I probably started in Sunday School when I was five years old. When I was in high school, I was in the choir. Reverend Sy Parsons was, I would say, worldly. What my folks thought of as an intelligent minister—they liked his preaching. He didn't dwell on the mystical aspects. He dwelled on the moral aspects and the lessons. My dad would talk with Reverend Parsons in the barber shop.

I enjoyed singing in the choir. We had our black robes and we would march in and march out. Now when I hear these hymns or whatever, I can sing along with them. My dad always felt that regardless of what your education or what your beliefs in religion turned out to be when you were older, it was a part of our history, part of our culture and it's good to know. You can believe what you want to believe as you grow older. That came from the Mennonite background. They believed that you shouldn't even be baptized until you're an adult and you make the decision, if that's what you want to do.

A LASTING IMPRESSION

I remember an Aunt Nell Rarden, or at least that's what we called her. She was a Sunday School teacher in the Congregational Church in Greenville. She put on little church plays that we did before the general church audience either for Christmas or some other festive occasion. At one time she had me play the part of Old Black Joe, an old black man dressed in tattered clothes, a cotton ball wig for gray hair and a cane, and I was bent over, and I sang the Negro spiritual "Old Black Joe." I think even then she was trying to get us to understand that all people of all races had feelings. And it would seem to me that in that sense she was the finest Sunday School teacher you could have, because I would hazard the guess that most Sunday School teachers don't leave lasting impressions like that with their students.

We are all products of our background

Mrs. W. L. Rarden introduced the ever-entertaining kindergarten program with a few well-chosen remarks. This program was charmingly staged and showed the results of long hours of patient training given the children.

"Pages from an Old Song Book" was the theme and gave the children a chance to depict many of the quaint characters of the earlier days. Every number was wonderful, going from the humorous to the sublime as the closing scenes brought the great congregation in prayer to the foot of the cross, the "Rock of Ages".

While each child gave their part of the program perfectly, special mention must be made of the work of little Frederick Meyers, who seemed to be the key lad around whom much of the work was centered. Frederick was equally as good in "Old Black Joe," "Your Highland Laddie," and "Barefoot Boy." The two songs were given in costume. Special mention must also be made of the number given by Miss Wanda Tuttle and Charles McLean, who sang the old-fashioned song, "Where Have You Been, Billy Bo?" in costume.

Old Santa arrived in the nick of time to the joy both of the children and the grown-ups. Three hundred oranges and boxes of candy disappeared like magic and undoubtedly in the great crowd some little folks were missed, but the spirit of Christmas prevailed, to be carried away in the hearts of everyone.

Fred as Old Black Joe in a Congregational church Christmas play.
The story at left notes that "special mention must be made of the work of little Frederick Meyers [sp]"

SEEDS OF REBELLION

I can remember the first set of skis I got for Christmas. I guess I got them the Christmas morning before my dad and I peddled milk, and I was 7 years old or so. We had Thorwald McFarland on the milk wagon with us, and the three of us were peddling milk on this Christmas morning. My dad was trying to be tricky with me. I peddled the milk to this customer's house up on the corner of 5th and Summit, someplace in there. So I knew we had to go another block or two up the street and then, as we came back, I was going to hop back on the wagon. But my dad made the horse go faster and faster and faster, and he knew that if I couldn't catch up with the horse, at least I could wait just a minute, and they'd pick me up again. But I got so furious that I just went home and let my dad and Thorwald peddle the milk. When I got home I put on my new Christmas skis and my dad was so mad he was going to smash them up. He was furious because I really called his bluff. It just shows that the seeds of rebellion are in many of us if they're brought out at the proper time, and I rebelled against my dad playing tricks on me.

SNOWED IN

I remember one time when we were snowed in. It was when we weren't using the horse to peddle milk anymore. We were using a cut down car of some kind, and the car wouldn't start or was stuck, so we peddled the whole milk route with a sled. A toboggan would have been much better, because the sled sank in and was very hard for my dad to pull. He just pulled his heart out, and I was pushing, and I was cold, and I was crying. My dad felt very sorry for me, but he said, "Fred, I'm cold too and as soon as we get this milk peddled, we can go home." But there was no way he could just abandon the milk and take me home, and he needed my help so he felt very sorry for me but we had to keep on peddling that milk. It's just one old memory you never forget.

Fred attended Pearl Street School, where he was a kindergartener sitting in front of Johanna at far right for this school picture

Young Fred's pose with a family cow c. 1927 was later reproduced as an Andre Harvey sculpture for the Frederik Meijer Gardens

THE SMART HORSE

I used to haul manure out to the farm. It took me all day to take a horse and wagon and spread the manure and then come back to Greenville with the horse and wagon. It was about five miles out in the country. We used to spread it by hand because we didn't have a manure spreader.

I used to mow hay. I was very good at repairing and replacing pittmans. A pittman is the wooden shaft that goes from the little fly wheel on the mowing machine to the cutter. It was made out of wood or metal, but when it was made out of wood, it was intentionally made so it would break if you hit something that would wreck the machine if it didn't break. We used to have to cut hay in an orchard on the farm, a stumped orchard, and every once in a while I'd hit something and it would break a pittman, and I'd replace it. But I rather enjoyed being able to replace the pittman. And we used to grind the mowing machine teeth on the grinder that we had to pump up and down with our feet--big flywheel grinders. The grinder itself was the flywheel.

We had a farmer who was working the farm. His name was Smith. My dad would take Mr. Smith out to the farm and one day he called up my dad to come and get him, because the horse was sick. That happened two, three days and finally my dad says to me, "You know, that horse, if it isn't well enough to work, why don't you try him out and see whether he's well this morning and then we'll have Mr. Smith go tomorrow." So I took the horse out, and he seemed all right. He'd go up and down the field a few times, and I'd rest him in the shade, and he'd lay down in the harness. I thought that was odd.

He always laid down in the shade. So when his knees started sagging in the shade, I just took a switch and kept him moving. I rested him in the middle of the field. That horse had just outsmarted the farmer. He found out that he could act sick and lay down in the shade and the farmer would give him the day off. So in my own kid fashion I wised up to the horse's trick.

HORSE TRADERS

We had all kinds of horse dealings. Being poor farmers, we traded horses probably 29 or 30 times and got cheated every time but just a few. We had all kinds of bad things with horses: spasms, sweeneys, sway back, club feet, cancer of the rectum, broken windpipe, heaves, kick in the harness, lay down in the harness, balk--you name it, we had it. We sure had a lot of lousy horses. As a matter of fact, we had so many bad horses that when I had to bring them home somebody would holler, "Oh, Henry bought another horse." They'd holler at me. I'd say yes, and I'd keep on riding him home.

"My dad thought I was old enough," said Fred later of his helping hay farmland north of Greenville

OLD ENOUGH

I hauled a load of hay home with one or two horses, I can't remember which, from Gowen, and my mother thought I was too young. My dad thought I was old enough. I thought I was old enough and I was so proud when I brought that load of hay into Greenville. My mother took my picture, and I think we still have a picture with me on the load of hay when I came into the yard.

CONSTIPATED HORSES

We had a horse that would kick in the middle of the night. We'd hear boom, boom, boom, boom, and he was kicking the stall. The horse had constipation, and my dad said,"that horse is going to die if he doesn't get a bowel movement." So he got me to ride the horse around the field in front of the house-- which is the parking lot of where the store now stands--and rode him round and round and round and finally I heard him pass some gas. It was a black horse, and it was black in the night but there were no trees in the field, and I just rode him at a slow trot or a gallop or a walk until finally we heard some bowel movement action. And then I took the horse back to the farm. The horse, as far as I know, lived happily ever after.

MY FIRST BIKE

My dad bought me my first bicycle for $5. My dad loved to paint, so we painted the bike all up and got it all fixed up. Then when I had the bike for a year or two, someone wanted to buy it. By that time I had a back carrier on it, a basket in the front, I had a light on it, and maybe it had a horn and a bell. It was pretty well ornamented. My dad said if you sell that bicycle for seven dollars and a half, I'll get you a new one. Well, the Depression was on about then. I took everything off and I knew the guy that wanted it and he just kept me putting stuff back on until I put on every lousy bell, whistle, carrier, basket. Everything that I ever put on it. Then I got my seven dollars and a half.

I got my seven dollars and a half, but too much time had elapsed. We were so doggone hard up that I didn't get another bicycle for two years. In high school the bicycle I got was from Sears Roebuck and we paid $17 for it. We paid a dollar down and a dollar a month.

FEET IN THE FLAKES

I used to study after school with my feet in a corn flakes box because the heat would die down in the evening in the kitchen, and that's the only heat we had in the house--we only heated one room. Sometimes on Sundays we would heat the rest of the house, but during the Depression when my folks went to bed and I had some studying to do, I would cover

Fred was born in a main-floor bedroom to the right in this farmhouse on Greenville's north side. Note from Hendrik to Fred's teacher explaining his son's absence: "We could not get the car started and the horse slipped on the ice, so we had all kinds of trouble"

myself with blankets and put a coat on. I wasn't that good a student, so I don't think I did it too often, but your mind has a way of thinking you did things you ought to do more times than you actually did them.

BOVINE LUCK

My dad tried to get into the dairy business, and that was a disaster. He tried registered guernsey cattle. He bought three registered heifers and had them bred, and one got into fresh alfalfa and bloated and died. One came in three-teated and the other one came in dry.

THE MODEL DAIRY

We couldn't sell milk to grocery stores when we were in the dairy business because we lost the bottles. The bottles just went out. We'd sell the milk for a nickel a quart and the bottles cost us a nickel. If we didn't get them back we were just giving the milk away. Now Blanding, Greenville's largest dairy, could afford to do that, because they had enough distribution so that if people bought the milk in the store and took it home, somehow the bottles would end up on somebody's porch, and Blanding would get back many more than we did proportionately.

Well, anyway, my dad wanted to sell Richmond, a grocer, our milk, and Fred Richmond said, "I'm paying Blanding 5 cents a quart, and selling for 6 cents a quart; I got to buy this milk for 4-1/2 cents a quart." My dad says, "My God man, we're going broke. Haven't you got any consideration?"

"I can't worry about your problem," Richmond says, "I got to buy it for 4-1/2 cents a quart. I need 1-1/2 cents a quart profit."

"Okay," my dad said, "I tell you what I'll do. If you will charge for the bottles and guarantee that I'll get the bottles back, I'll sell it to you for 4-1/2 a quart." And Richmond said "That's fine." So, my dad went to Wood Printing and had $2.27 worth of tickets made. I only know that figure because my dad cried about it for 30 years. He had the tickets printed so that every time someone bought a bottle of milk they got a ticket. It was the best system we could think of. They might buy the milk at the house and bring to the store and sell our bottle for a nickel.

Well, then, after we had all the tickets made, Fred Richmond said, "I'm sorry, but I can't bother with the tickets and charging for the milk." So we lost the $2.27.

Fred and friend Thorwald "Dusty" McFarland peddled milk from door to door on a cart drawn by this pony

LEGAL NOTICE

Having registered by name "Model Dairy" (H. Meyer) under the provisions of Act. 36, Public Acts of 1927,

It will therefore be unlawful for any person to use my bottles, containers, etc.

H. Meyer,
Model Dairy,
Greenville, Mich.

Notice of name registration for Hendrik's "Model Dairy" venture in 1928

As we were moving the equipment into the Greenville store, we were the laughing stock of the community for even going into the grocery business. It might have been Mrs. Richmond who walked by going from downtown to North Greenville, and she says, "Oh, so you're going in the grocery business, huh?"

My dad says, "Yes, you remember the time that you had to have a cent and a half on each quart of milk we were selling you? You said you couldn't worry about us, you had to worry about your part of the business? Well, I want to get on that side of the business then." And we did. But my dad was always kind of unhappy that they wouldn't use our tickets. So we got out of the milk business finally and we're in the grocery business.

I can also remember when Kipp was a customer in my dad's barbershop and my mother would ask what could you buy something for at A&P. I was never, never in an A&P. We never bought a nickel's worth of stuff at A&P all the time that my dad was in the barbershop. We bought a lot of stuff in A&P afterwards, while we were price shopping them, but that was after we were in the business. In the barbershop days, we were loyal to our barbershop customer's grocery business.

MY FIRST RECITAL

I took music lessons a good many years. I took piano lessons when I was five or six years old. Never did learn much. I couldn't remember my first recital piece, so I played half of it and forgot the rest. I ended up singing the other half.

SUCKING LEMONS

I remember sitting behind the cook stove in the old house. It was nice and warm back there. My sister liked to suck on lemons and she liked sour lemons. If I had to suck on a lemon, I'd put sugar on it. That's what's wrong with my teeth now.

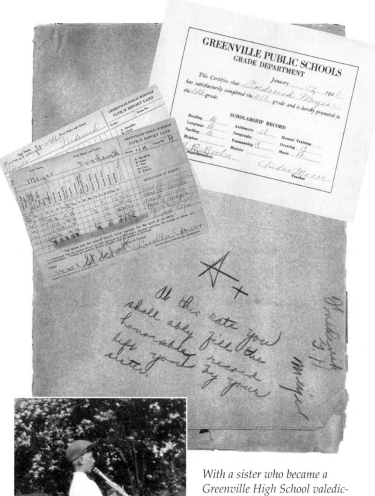

With a sister who became a Greenville High School valedictorian, Fred followed in studious footsteps, as suggested by the comment above from one of his teachers

Raised by parents keenly interested in music, Fred studied piano, violin and clarinet

IT'S A STUPID RULE

I can remember a time in high school when we were not supposed to go to lockers between classes. Miss Lou, our teacher, was trying to enforce the locker rule. We had Latin right after lunch, and she said to each one of us, "Do you have all your books?" "Yes, Miss Lou," we said. She asked the next one, do you have all your books? Yes, Miss Lou.

They were all lying. None of them had all their books for the afternoon. She got to me and asked, "Do you have all your books, Fred?" "No, Miss Lou." "You don't have all your books? You know what the rules are." "Yes, Miss Lou. " "Don't you think you ought to go get the books?" "No, Miss Lou." "Why not?" "Because I think it's a stupid rule. And nobody's abiding by it, and I think it's wrong."

"Well," she says, "I'm the teacher and I'm supposed to enforce it, and you ought to go get your books. Please go get them." I said, "No Miss Lou, I'm not going to get them. I think the rule is wrong." So she went on around the room and everybody else said, we're not going to get in that trap, "Yes, Miss Lou, yes, Miss Lou." Well, anyway, when she came to hand out the marks, I was bad enough in Latin, but I always had good citizenship. She gave me a poor citizenship mark.

I went to see her and she says, "Well, Fred, you know that we had that locker rule, and even though it was rescinded a few days later, you should have gone. You should have gone. It was the rule, and you should have abided by it." I said "I thought the rule was stupid, and I didn't think I should."

"Well," she says, "I thought you should. Therefore, I gave you a bad mark. But if you feel that you understand it well enough now, I'll change your card to a better citizenship mark." I said, "No, you don't have to," and I wheeled and walked out of the room. And I was really being kind of nasty then. I think she liked me, and I think I left her in tears because she didn't want me to have a bad citizenship mark, but she was kind of trapped.

I shouldn't have done what I did, and my conscience still bothers me a little bit, but it just demonstrates to me how you can make a rebel out of anybody if you have the right situation, and it's better not to make rebels out of people. It's better to try to figure out some way to accommodate their feelings and also not throw out all the rules.

CHAPTER 2

~

THE 30s

With love from Johanna and Freddie.

STARTING OUT

My dad and I ran all over trying to rent the storefront. If I was out of school, I went with him. He went to A&P and Kroger--this would probably be in the fall of 1933. He couldn't rent it. He went to see about another chain, C. Thomas, that had a store in Ionia. Mr. Thomas never even looked up, just said, "not interested."

So then he went to Lee and Cady, which he heard owned a chain of Red and White stores. Lee and Cady said they supplied independent grocers. Red and White stores were their co-operative buying group. So when we started the store, I think it was Lee and Cady's idea. They said, if your credit is good we'll loan you the groceries on some basis, and so they went to Mr. Ranney and Mr. Ranney said, "Hey, Henry Meijer's going to go broke in the grocery business, but somehow he will pay you back."

The store was only 21 feet wide and 70 feet long. The building was raw studding. You stood inside it and the outside surface was on, but the inside wasn't finished, so in the spring of '34 my dad bought used lath. You buy a bundle, probably, for a nickel. Lath is something like a yard stick, with plaster on it. My job coming home after high school was to chip off the old plaster, taking out the nails, straightening the nails and then nailing them onto the 2 x 4s. I'm sure I did a very small part of the lathing. Yet maybe I did more than I realized. I would do that every night and on Saturdays.

You had to leave a gap of about a quarter of an inch, and you'd put a block of lath up and then you'd stagger a block of lath so that you didn't have a straight line because you might get a crack in the plaster. My dad still didn't have the money to pay a plasterer, so he hired a plasterer for $10, payable via a violin that was supposedly worth $10. The plasterer wanted the violin; we wanted the plaster job. I remember the plasterer's name real well. It was Mr. O'Dell. He said, just remember, "Oh Hell." That was a radical word in those days, and I never forgot Mr. O'Dell. I helped him somewhat with the plaster, mixing or handing him a bucket which he dumped on a mortar board. Did I help a lot or a little? I think I helped a lot, but you know kids' memories.

We started out as North Side Grocery. Then we became Red

Toothpicks and Wheaties are among the items listed on the invoice of June 20, 1934 that accompanied Hendrik's first order of groceries. The bill came to $328.76

and White. I'll never forget how the back room of the store wasn't insulated. It was darn cold. All there was were roof boards with tar paper over them, and you could see frost on all the nails. So we insulated the underside of the rafters with cardboard that we got off the cartons from Lee and Cady. When Lee and Cady sold us groceries, they gave us $200 to $250 worth on credit, but from then on they said, "Everything is cash." So they wrote "cash" on every case in blue chalk, and when you looked up at our back room ceiling, it said cash, cash, cash, cash, cash all over.

Anyway, now that we are a Red and White Store and advertising with the two stores downtown, the two stores downtown complained: it isn't right that another Red and White store undersells us on milk. And so the Red and White Lee and Cady representative came and told my dad, "You've got to raise that milk price," and my dad says, "I can't raise that milk price. I can't get rid of the milk if I do. I charge for the bottle and it's raw milk." They said, "you've go to." My dad says, " I can't." Well, they said, "you've either got to or we've got to take that Red and White sign down."

"Well, then we'll have to take the sign down." My dad went out in the back room and got the ladder, and he and the Red and White man took the Red and White sign down.

OUR FIRST CUSTOMER

Even though Ellis Ranney was opposed to us going into the grocery business, when we opened the first store, he came in and said, "Brother I want to be your first customer." I started to say "Mr. Ranney, you can't be. I've already sold some tobacco and candy to someone else."

And my dad practically kicked me in the pants and said "Shut up. He wants to be the first customer. He's the first customer." And I think Mr. Ranney understood the byplay because it all happened right in front of him, so I said, "Oh, excuse me, Mr. Ranney, here you are,"--whatever it was-- "you're our first customer."

BAD COFFEE

On the grand opening day we served Green & White coffee, and the man who was demonstrating the coffee said, "Now, when this runs out, you just put the coffee in here and a pail of water in here and let it perk"--or boil or whatever coffee does in one of those big urns--"and then you'll be all set to go." I did that, and I served it to a lot of people. They were all too polite to tell me it was terrible. Finally my dad came up from the barbershop, and I gave him a cup of coffee, and he says, "My gosh, what kind of slop you got there? Dump it out. Dump it out." So that was my first experience in making coffee, on a big quantity, and it was terrible.

PAINTING SIGNS

Back in the days of the first store, I painted signs in the basement with water colors on white butcher paper. Before that I learned to paint with whiting. That's a kind of a chalky powder that you mix with water on the store windows. The problem with whiting was that when there was a good rain, the stuff all ran off because you painted it on the outside. When you had the signs on the inside, that worked better because you could hang them up and the rain or the wind wouldn't ruin the sign.

Fred paints weekly specials in the front window of the North Side Grocery, c. 1935

MR. RANNEY'S RECEIPTS

One time Ellis Ranney came in the store and he said, "Why should I buy from you folks for cash when I can buy just as cheap from Svenson (a competitor) and get it delivered?" I said, "Mr. Ranney, bring me some of your credit tapes." So he brought them. I've got them yet, by the way--those little tickets. He brought them in and threw them on the counter, and said he couldn't save much. So I proceeded to figure them out--what we would have charged for them.

He says, "Well, there's only 75 cents difference."

I said, "Gee, Mr. Ranney--it's 15 percent. That's a lot of money." That sold him. He was a banker.

BUYING COD

In the early days we thought we would order a big order from the wholesaler and get it on credit. But they sent it up COD, and we were in trouble. I said to my dad, "What do I do? The order came COD." My dad said, "I don't know. Unload it and we'll worry about it afterwards. At least we'll get it unloaded and see what happens."

But they were short a case or two, and the truck driver and I couldn't find that case. He got so mad being short a case or two--at himself, not at us, but just mad. He jumped in the cab, and he says, "Just sign it, deduct the case," which we did, and he jumped into the truck and took off.

About an hour later, Jo from Grand Rapids Wholesale called me up and said, "Didn't you know that was a COD order?" I said, "Yeah, we did, but the driver took off and didn't get his money." "Well, what are we going to do about it?"

"Well, we'll be in Monday morning." This might have been either Thursday or Friday. And so Monday morning we went in with--let's say the order was $600, I don't remember the amount--and if we took in $400 over the weekend, we brought them all the money we had and then gave her a check for the other $200 or so. In those days the checks went to Chicago from Grand Rapids and then back to Greenville, and it took 3 or 4 days. By the time the check got back, why then we had it covered.

When our checks bounced, Jo really worked us over. We thought she was tough, but we also respected her--when we had a chance to hire her brother as our meat director, we wanted him because we felt if he's half as good as his sister, he ought to be a good man. It was good judgment. It worked out fine.

THE SPELLING

John Lewis was a Greenville attorney. He was responsible for us using the name M-e-i-j-e-r instead of M-e-y-e-r because he wrote our name on some legal paper M-y-e-r-s; also M-e-y-e-r; also M-e-i-j-e-r; and that is when dad said well, let's pick the one that was on my naturalization papers and my passport, and that was M-e-i-j-e-r.

Hendrik (left) and cafe proprietor Pat McCann in a doorway dynamited through a basement wall of the Thrift Market in 1937

DYNAMITE DOWNSTAIRS

In 1936 we bought the building next door and we needed a door from the outside so we could build an outside stairway entrance to the basement. Dad hired one fellow for $10 to cut a hole in the wall. He worked and worked and worked, then he gave up. So, Dad hired another fellow for $10, same thing. So he hired a third man, named Rudy Swartz, to put a hole in the wall--right below where we were checking out customers. Then all at once the building shook a little, we heard a tink and a rattle and another tink and a rattle. Then Rudy comes up and says, "Well Henry, you owe me $10."

He had blasted the whole doorway out with dynamite. Dynamite! Right while we were doing business upstairs. It's a good thing he knew what he was doing, or he would have blown up the place.

NOBODY SAID LIFE WAS FAIR

I had a teacher in Greenville--Larry Robinson--who had a lot of opinions on a lot of subjects, and his opinions must have affected me because I have quoted from them, and I have remembered them. For instance, one of his thoughts was that the reason Jewish people are so smart is because they were so persecuted that they had to be smart just to stay alive, and the ones who weren't quite as clever or smart got killed off. I don't necessarily buy all that, but that was one of the things I remember him saying. I also remember that because we were in the dairy business, I was saying that butter is wonderful, and it's sort of full of food value and oleomargarine has no food value. In those days oleomargarine was not much different than lard only made out of vegetables. But he challenged me on it and said oleomargarine does have food value. Even lard, as a fat, has food value.

I can remember another time when Mr. Robinson had a test, and he asked us how many of us thought the test was unfair and many of us thought the test was unfair. Well, he says, that's good because you're going to find out when you get out of high school that nothing is really fair. You might as well start learning it now. We thought that maybe he would tear up the test and throw it in the waste basket because we thought it was unfair, but he certainly made a point. At least he made a point with me.

When one of his students was all for the Republicans, he'd jump on the Democratic side. If he had one who was Democratic, he'd jump on the Republican side. If he'd get a good argument going between a kid who was a Republican and one who was a Democrat, he'd take the Socialist side. And so he constantly endeavored to make you think, and what more can a good teacher do but express challenging views, leave lasting thoughts and get you to think? I've always admired his teaching ability for that. He was the one teacher who had the most effect on me. Maybe if I'd gone to the university, I would have placed him amongst several other fine examples, but because I did not, I hold him out as one of the best examples of a teacher.

TEACHERS CALL THEM.	WE CALL THEM	CHERISHED POSSESSION	HOBBY	HOPES TO BE	ALWAYS SEEN WITH
Virginia Butts	- Buttsy	Icky Louse sweater	Chewing Gum	School Teacher	Roselan Moyer
Alton Cairns	Carrots	Cane	Giving Away Candy	Band Leader	Joe Eichelberg
Lemiux	Jerry	Shoes	Pastry Slinger	Model	Madeline Slocum
Fred Meijers	Fritz	Milk Can	Delivering Milk	Doctor Yank Emont	Robert Keyt
Roselen Moyer				Kindergarten	Virginia

"Fritz Meijers'" cherished possession was a milk can, according to this Greenville High School yearbook

PRACTICAL THINKING

Mr. Robinson said we wouldn't have any racial problems if everybody was intermarried and all the white people were a little darker and black people were a little lighter. Then we wouldn't look at each other as being different.

I also remember the records of Carl Sandburg, "The People, Yes," where he talks about our prejudices and our prides and our reactions between the races and nationalities. It left a tremendous impression on me. I still have three sets of those records at home, and in their treatment of prejudice and human dignity and feelings, they're as up-to-date now as they were 40 years ago when I first heard them.

You must respect yourself to have others respect you

FRED'S DIARY

SATURDAY, FEBRUARY 15, 1936
*Pa painted almost all day. Ma washed, so I worked 15 hours in the
store. (We joined the AG stores and have to paint the store cream
and green.)*

SATURDAY, APRIL 4, 1936
*Bought two horses today, one for $75 and one for $40. The $75 one is
four years old this May. It has coon feet. The other is 14 years old
and limps a bit so we have a good cripple team. (All we need is
crutches.)*

TUESDAY, JULY 21, 1936
*We had ensemble practice. We got our "Thrift Market" neon sign
yesterday. I piled goods out on the sidewalk for the first time today. I
think it looks okay.*

MONDAY, SEPTEMBER 28, 1936
*School is sure giving me plenty of work this year. We are going to fix
a stove in the back of the store so I can practice and study.*

SUNDAY, OCTOBER 18, 1936
*I studied tonight. Pa and I went to the show this afternoon at
Silvers, "The Gorgeous Hussy" with Robert Taylor, etc. It was a
story taking place in Jackson's time. England said yesterday she
wanted (I forget just how many thousands) men to go to school to
learn to teach all their women and children how to use gas masks.*

SATURDAY, OCTOBER 31, 1936
*J.D. Rockefeller, H. Ford, J.P. Morgan are all for Landon. We had a
good day in store today. We heard both Roosevelt and Landon give
their final speeches tonight. Roosevelt said he hated war and would
continue to keep the country safe from war. He also said the "money
class" hated him, but that he welcomed their hate. Landon gave a
weak speech. Landon sure is no orator, but Roosevelt is an excellent
one.*

WEDNESDAY, NOVEMBER 4, 1936
12:30 a.m. Pa and Ma's 24th wedding anniversary. We had a speech

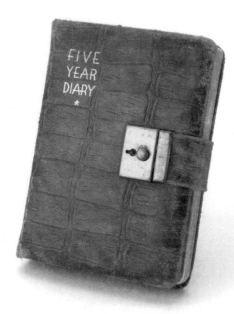

Fred's teenaged diary blended notes about world events on the eve of World War II with an account of day-to-day activity in the family's Thrift Market

by the new Methodist minister today. I thought the speech was a very narrow-minded one. He said all foreigners who tried to stir up trouble or were radical should be sent back and that he hoped the ship would sink with them on the way back. Pa was fined $10 yesterday by a federal man because he forgot to scratch a wine stamp. That sure is justice, isn't it.

THURSDAY, NOVEMBER 26, 1936
12:10 Thanksgiving. Business was not very good either today or yesterday. Pa and I went to Gibsons tonight and saw Will Rogers in "State Fair" with Janet Gaynor. I have seen it twice now, but it sure is a good show. Ma has not felt at all well today, she has been feverish. Even after she agreed to stay in bed, she got up and worked on relief orders. We are sure getting a lot of them lately.

WEDNESDAY, DECEMBER 2, 1936
We made out an ad tonight. We are going to put in HOT specials every week now instead of every day prices. Sis sent us another letter today for $15 to have her teeth fixed with. I have been studying tonight and can hardly keep awake to write this. I handed in an Eng. Lit. theme today.

MASS MERCHANT

Long before he got into the grocery business, when my dad had the barbershop, he would tell people about the Food City Discount Supermarket in Grand Rapids and the T.C. DeYoung Meat Market, and how the people from up and down Charles Street, in Greenville, would go to Grand Rapids to buy there. And he told this to the local merchants like Mr. Kipp, and Mr. Kipp said, "Henry, you look after the barber business, and we'll look after the grocery business."

When we went to Grand Rapids to visit these stores, my dad and me, I can well remember the first customer that came out of T.C. DeYoung's Cut Rate Meat Market was a night watchman from the Ranney Refrigerator Company factory in Greenville. And then we went over to the Food City stores to see what they were doing and they, too, had customers from our hometown of Greenville.

BEING COMPETITIVE

Kroger wasn't as competitive as A&P. They used to run hot specials and have their own private label, but when A&P went supermarket, A&P became devilishly competitive. We went right down the line with them, and it was good for us that we did. But we were only able to do it because my dad and mother and I, and earlier my sister, were working in the store, and we furnished probably three quarters of the labor for a long time. As we grew bigger we couldn't, but it sure became the basis to keep our overhead down. When A&P had to hire all the labor and our time wasn't worth that much, we could be competitive.

USE THRIFT MARKET LANGUAGE

One day my dad sent me to the bank. As I walked in, the banker asked me how the weather was outside.

Since it was an especially nice day, and I had just learned a new word that expressed how I was feeling, I replied, "Invigorating."

The banker said to me in a serious tone, "Fred, why don't you use Thrift Market language."

I always resented his "put down" reply.

The Thrift Market touts low prices and its switch to cash-selling in this newspaper ad from October 1936. Decades later the stores would again be open "Sundays, evenings and holidays." Below, 16-year old Fred notes the varied course of his father's career with these notations on Hendrik's letterhead

OVERBUYING

We were constantly overbuying--doing things like, "Okay, if it's $2 a dozen for your normal list price, could you sell it to us for $1.90 if we bought 10 cases?" If the vendor said, "Yeah I'll give you $1.90," we'd say, "Well, what if we bought 100, would you give it to us for $1.80?" If he said "yes" we'd probably buy the darn 100 for $1.80 and so forth.

WE CAN EAT IT

I remember when a customer brought back a 10-cent package of a rice krispy type of cereal. It was A&P's type of rice krispy and said right across the bottom the Great Atlantic and Pacific Tea Company. He says, "My wife got this here. It's the wrong thing and we want our money back." I started to point out to the man, "Sir, you couldn't have bought that here. This says Atlantic and Pacific," and my dad says, "Keep still. Give the man his 10 cents back for what he bought here." Then he hauled me off to one side, and he said, "Listen, we can eat it. Don't send him to A&P for a dime when we can eat the A&P rice krispies." So that's how we developed our refund policies, most of which are still in effect today.

KNIFE-DODGING BUTCHER

When we had just one store we had a meat man named Einar Jorgensen, and we had gone to White Cloud and bought our first walk-in cooler. It was a used cooler, and we took it down in sections and brought it in on a truck. I remember going up the hill in Newaygo and being afraid as we followed it with a car that those sections of the cooler would slide off and slide all the way down the hill. They did not. But this man who had the truck was named George, and I think he was slightly simple or not quite all there, but he had the truck and did trucking like that. We found an old knife up in White Cloud--George is pretty good at throwing knives--so when we got back into Greenville, I said to George, show Einar how well you can throw a knife. George is pretty good at hitting a target with that knife, and we had a wooden wall in back, and I really thought maybe he would just toss the knife toward that wall. But we also had some beef hanging in front of it, so he picks up a knife from behind the meat case, goes around in front of the meat case, and here is Einar Jorgensen in between the sides of beef that he's going to throw the knife into. And this guy is swinging this knife around. I can remember Einar getting down on his hands and knees--I would have done the same thing, he'd be crazy not to--and crawling along the floor because he was afraid that this George was going to throw the knife and maybe hit him. And George did throw the knife and stuck it into the beef, and then Einar got up off his hands and knees. It sure was funny. But that knife waving around didn't look funny to Einar.

PEACH KINGS

Johanna ran the store the first year and a half, from the last of June till September of the following year, 1935, when she went to the University of Michigan.

We had many experiences running that store. One was buying by objectives. A peddler peach trucker came to Greenville and offered to sell us peaches at 45 cents a bushel. They were called gold drops, and he said he'd be there Friday afternoon

The Thrift Market crew in this 1935 photo includes Hendrik, Johanna and Fred (second from right)

so we could sell them Saturday morning. We ran an ad in the Friday night paper advertising "gold drop peaches in your own container" for 50 cents a bushel.

That Friday night the peddler didn't show up, and my dad and I were desperate for peaches, so we took our truck and went to Grand Rapids on the market early Saturday morning. By the time we got back (by the way, this was our first experience in buying on the market in Grand Rapids), here was the man that was supposed to come Friday. So now we had two loads of peaches. By golly, we sold out both those loads between 8 a.m. and noon. That showed us that we could sell peaches, and from then on, our objective was to beat the A&P price on peaches--have them a little riper, ready to can--and we used to sell 100 bushels to the A&P store's 5 or 10 bushels, once we got rolling. For a while, we were the peach kings of Montcalm County.

THURSDAY, JANUARY 28, 1937

I finished the ad this morning. I have been carrying stuff up from the cellar all day and pricing it as fast as Dorothy put it on the shelf. Pa almost finished one side of the partition of the ice box. I painted some posters for the windows this afternoon.

WEDNESDAY, FEBRUARY 3, 1937

I tried out for the senior play again, I do not know whether or not I will get a part, but all I can do is hope. I made out an ad for tomorrow's Daily. We bought a soap deal tonight from Swift with which we get a grocery and meat sign with a neon light surrounding it.

THURSDAY, FEBRUARY 4, 1937

I could not sleep well thinking about the play last night. I could not study the first hour this morning. In home room the cast was announced. In the play cast are Fred Meijer, Ed Sharp, E. Carins, W. Walker, H. Kingsbury, Joy Sheldon, Marvel Rasmussen, Louise Kennedy and Dorothy Krass. I got the part of a young "painter" and "lover."

MONDAY, FEBRUARY 8, 1937

I got up at 5:40 this morning, finished my English Lit. theme and made a report for English Lit. I had 4 hours and 20 minutes sleep last night. We got our play books for the Senior Play. I am definitely cast as Warren, a young painter and lover.

THURSDAY, FEBRUARY 25, 1937

Because so many sit down strikes are going on, we headed our ad "Sit Down Strikers will get up for these prices." I went to Grand Rapids and saw "Late C. Bean." The whole cast went except H. Kingsbury. Gander, Mary Pearl, Bud Svensen, Miss Eldred and Miss Petersen also went. Saw Gerald Kegstra.

THURSDAY, MARCH 11, 1937

We got our 5 week marks today. I got A- in English Lit from Garder, B in U.S. History from Rugy, A in Comm. Law from Dibble, B+ in Business English from Miss Clark. Pa's fixing an office over the stairway. I helped some tonight. We had play practice tonight. The first time I have had to kiss Dorothy. I could not do it on the stage so we had to go to the back and practice, after that I had to do it twice on the stage.

Fred graduated from Greenville High School in 1937 after appearing in the senior play, one of his few extra-curricular activities

SCHOOL DAYS

I can remember trying to learn to dance and then going to a high school dance and asking a girl to dance. It was a disaster. She just quit and walked off. I don't blame her much. Her name was Marvel Rasmussen. But anyway, if you couldn't make it work, you couldn't make it work, so I guess I should not have blamed her. Later on she was in a school play with me.

I can remember the school play in high school real well. I was the boyfriend and Dorothy Krass was the girl friend. I couldn't kiss her, and I had to as part of the play, so they sent us in the back of the room to practice. Finally she said, if you don't like it, you don't have to do it. Well, I was just so embarrassed, I could hardly do it.

I never went to a football game or a basketball game all the time I was in high school because I was always needed in the store. The minute school was done, I would hurry to the store and work there till it closed at 10:00 or 10:30 or 11:00. I think we usually closed at 10:00, but it took half an hour or so to get out. On Saturdays till 11:30, and then we were open Sundays until we could afford to be closed Sundays.

MONDAY, MARCH 22, 1937
We had play practice tonight. We sent in Grand Rapids Wholesale order. Pa was in Grand Rapids today and bought a new meat grinder, a cooler, some coils, 2 sets of scales - 1 candy scale and a fruit scale. He also paid up the Wholesalers.

MONDAY, JULY 12, 1937
Pa, Ma, and I went to Big Rapids today and looked at a large A&P self-serve there. It was about the first in Michigan. We also drove by Ox Bow "Hardy" and other dams. We came home around by Newaygo to see the sights along the Muskegon river.

TUESDAY, JULY 13, 1937
Pa and I worked next door until 3:00 p.m. Then we went to Grand Rapids with the grocery order and took A&P measurements at Grandville Avenue store. Then we drove in rain to Muskegon and saw Food City and peeked through window at A&P.

MONDAY, AUGUST 2, 1937
I took down the north wall shelves today while pa painted. We hung the new "Thrift Market" sign tonight, I was on the roof and pulled up one end with a rope. There were four of us with ropes from the roof and four men shoved up from the bottom. It sure is a beautiful sign.

THURSDAY, AUGUST 12, 1937
Worked in store all day. We closed this afternoon, but worked (after a short nap) just the same. We put in the new counter and took out the old ones. I think we have got the tables in the north side of the store adjusted just about right. We have been getting up early and work-ing late every night. Today was 7:15 a.m. until 11:30 p.m.

FRIDAY, AUGUST 13, 1937
We have got Edna K. sacking and Pa and I are fixing the counter into place while Ma, Sister, Dorothy S. sweep and wait on trade. We sent in grocery order for Monday. Monday we will start packing the stock in place for good. We hope to open next Saturday.

WEDNESDAY, AUGUST 18, 1937

We got a $350 dollar order from Grand Rapids Wholesale. I have been pricing, packing and painting. I painted the self-serve ammonia case tonight. Ma and Sis packed a big supply of cookies onto tables. I made out the opening ad today. We open next Saturday. I guess Dorothy S. quit last night. We worked until 12:00 tonight.

THURSDAY, AUGUST 19, 1937

The ad (full page) $40 came out today. It sure looks swell. We also put a full page ad in the Buyers Guide. We hired Alva Hansen today, he did very good today. I have been pricing all day today. The Ammonia case man had trouble, ammonia leaked out and drove us all out. We worked until 12:30 tonight.

SUNDAY, AUGUST 22, 1937

Pa, Ma, Sis, Alva Hansen and I worked in the store all morning. We had a good morning for a Sunday. I believe the store is going to be enjoyable to work in from now on. Now we can go ahead and put the finishing touches on it.

SATURDAY, SEPTEMBER 4, 1937

We had a very good day today despite the fact that the new A&P just opened. We took in $365 in grocery, and $181 in meat. I had to get 400 pounds of sugar from A. Svensen because we ran out. The A&P said they were out and Erikson would not let us have any.

THURSDAY, SEPTEMBER 9, 1937

The ad came out today. We were lower than either A&P or Kroger. We ran a 1/2 page ad. I have been painting signs ever since we opened the store again this afternoon. Sis and I went up town to Don Farmer's new shoe store and I bought a pair of shoes ($4.95, size 11.)

FRIDAY, SEPTEMBER 10, 1937

I painted signs this morning. I have got the windows so plastered you can hardly see in. Pa, Einar and I visited the new master A&P. I cut down some long benches and put them in front of the fruit stand to set onions and crates on. We worked only until 10:30.

*The planned opening of a new A&P supermarket September 1, 1937
inspired the Meijer family to gear up for intense price competition*

A&P

We knew A&P was coming with a supermarket into
Greenville, and so when they did come, with exactly the same
style shelving as ours, we had people who would say, "Isn't
that something, A&P copied your shelving," and my dad said,
"Yeah, that's something."

But actually we'd copied theirs. Once we decided that we
wanted to be competitive we had to meet A&P. They came out
with just hundreds of everyday low prices, and no specials,
and we copied them. I have one of the ads in the office you
can see now. It's posted on the wall. We just put hundreds of
prices in the ad, or at least dozens--I think 5 and 6 to the column inch is a lot of prices, very fine print. But we wanted to
meet them (A&P) down the line. We worked very hard to do
that, and that was the basis that we built our business on.

An ad from August 1937 heralds the opening of a doubled-in-size Thrift Market on the eve of A&P's arrival

HE'S GOING BROKE

Back in the days of the Greenville store, we had the biggest meat counter in Montcalm County, five 10-foot meat cases from A&P's used salvage lot for $25 apiece. A&P had two new cases but we had five used ones, and we had a mass display, and they had a small display.

I can remember going up to Mount Pleasant once when a fellow named Harold Houseman opened a new store, and my dad said, "He's going broke," and I said, "Well, he might go broke."

"You don't know that, dad."

"He's going to go broke."

"How can you say that?"

"Well, he bought all that equipment on credit." And I said, "Well, we bought all our equipment on credit, too."

He said, "Yes, but ours was used and it didn't take us long to pay off. He bought it new, and he isn't gonna be able to stand the overhead." Well, he went broke.

TUESDAY, SEPTEMBER 28, 1937
I took my music lesson today and we had ensemble. I was promoted into the 1st violin section. The clerks had a meeting and went to see Fred Richmond and by talking very plain, persuaded him to close Thursday afternoons. The Social Security man was at the store. I have to fill out 27 blanks. We had never sent in our Social Security before.

FRIDAY, NOVEMBER 19, 1937
I made more price tags today and painted some signs. Pa and I went to a pancake supper tonight given by Cass St. PTA at Masonic Hall. We are selling Swift milk 64 cents a case below cost. We put on a 4 can limit (5 cents per can). It is sure funny to see how the people try to sneak 2 batches. We caught Emerald Perry and Guss Vogel trying to buy milk a second time.

TUESDAY, DECEMBER 14, 1937
I worked in the store on the ad this morning. We are advertising 160 articles in grocery and produce. We are running a 5 column ad in the Daily News and a one page ad in the Buyers Guide. Pa and I went to Grand Rapids today to the Veltman Cookie Co. and to Ionia to a flour mill.

TUESDAY, JANUARY 4, 1938
Pa and I went to Ionia and got flour today and we went on to Grand Rapids (with trailer) and paid Grand Rapids Wholesale Grocery Co. $42 and got a $201.00 order. We saw Muller about the bread man (Jack) and we went to Swift & Co. Swift raised the oleo another 1/2 cent to 11 1/2 so we did not take their oleo, but got some from Good Luck Foods for 10 1/2 cents.

SATURDAY, MARCH 12, 1938
Worked in store all day. We took in $448 today. It was an all time record. Hitler went to Austria today. He now has complete control.

THURSDAY, APRIL 7, 1938
Pa and I went to Grand Rapids today and took down 200 pecks of potatoes and took out a grocery order. We went to the Morton Hotel and made a deal with the Staley Starch man. We also saw a new Kroger store and "Shopper's Trading Post."

The Thrift Market began to look like a supermarket in 1937 when it was expanded to span two storefronts

WEDNESDAY, APRIL 13, 1938
Pa and I made the 2 ads, they sure are hot. Mother and I made out the Grand Rapids Wholesale order tonight. We had the grocery carts fixed so the baskets would fit in them length ways. ($2.00 each)

THURSDAY, MAY 19, 1938
Pa and I went to Grand Rapids and brought home the largest trailer order we have ever had...$481.00. We had a flat in the rain. It was a regular cloud burst tonight. We have got the load of groceries in the Ford garage. The carpenter took out the old stairway today going down, and put in a sub-floor.

WEDNESDAY, JUNE 22, 1938
I make out ads and part of order. Commercial Bank would not finance the truck we want to buy from Kingsbury. Pa and I worked until 12 o'clock turning the meat cases into new position.

THURSDAY, AUGUST 25, 1938
We went to Grand Rapids and got a $479 order and 5 barrels of vinegar from Van's and produce. We had a flat tire just out of Grand Rapids and had to call Eddie with Einar's truck to take off part of the load and help us change. We just got unloaded when it started to rain.

THURSDAY, SEPTEMBER 29, 1938
We got up at 4:30 a.m. this morning. We were in Grand Rapids Wholesale at 6:00 a.m. and then went on the market. This is the first time we have bought vegetables (other than the time we bought 50 bushels peaches.) We were home with the load of grocery and vegetables at 10 minutes to noon.

WEDNESDAY, OCTOBER 5, 1938
We made out both the order and the ad today. Tomorrow we are going on the market again. We had the "Thrift Market" name painted on the truck today.

HAULING GROCERIES

We used to haul groceries with a four-wheel big trailer that we bought used. It originally came from Montgomery Ward. And we had a 1937 Ford, so it had to be after 1937 I'm talking about. No brakes on the trailer, and I remember hauling up and down these steep hills like on 131 at Porter Hollow--the old road--and then coming up on what is now M-57 just east of the old 131--another high hill. We had to go like the dickens downhill in order to make the hill going up it, and it worked fine.

We hauled the groceries for months or a year or whatever it was. We had the trailer hitched to the car with a ball hitch, and then we had a couple of chains hooked around the car and around the two irons that went off on an angle from the car, and it never occurred to us that if the ball broke off, everything was centered at one spot and the irons or the steel rods or strapping would separate. The chains wouldn't be any protection at all. Well, we were coming into Greenville, and I can remember it was a graduation night so I was already out of high school. I graduated in 1937 so this must have been in June of 1939. All at once I look around and here's the trailer coming up along side of me. The ball had broken off, but I didn't notice when it jerked loose. The steel angle irons that we had the chains wrapped around separated and so there were no safety chains on the trailer, and the trailer was just slowly coming up along side of me--just starting to go down

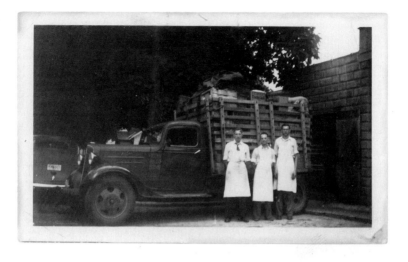

*Fred (left), with Marvin Petersen (right) and another co-worker,
was the Meijer grocery's first truck driver*

the hill toward the river. I can remember gently steering the
car into it. We, of course, wrecked the fender, tipping the trail-
er--forcing it to tip over--and by golly, we didn't lose over 50
cents worth of merchandise. Nothing broke, everything was
so gentle, but I could just see this picking up speed and going
into the river.

From then on I could never bring myself to haul that four-
wheel trailer. I could hardly even bring myself to haul it
empty. We had it fixed up, and we hauled it downtown and
sold it, and that's the last we ever used a trailer to haul groceries. We went from there to our first truck. That was a
straight dual-wheel truck, and then later on we went to a semi
and semis. Then when we got our first new truck, I was the
only one who was supposed to drive it because that was a
tremendous investment and nobody else should drive it. Now
we get semis, and most of them I've never even sat in much
less driven. But in those days that was such a big investment
to us that we couldn't have anybody but Fred drive that truck.
He would be careful with it. He knew what it cost.

SELF SERVICE

Ellis Ranney, who had endorsed our mortgages and was taking some of our debts out in due bills, said to me, "Freddy" or "brother" or whatever he called me (it was probably "brother"), "You talk about going to self service. If you will get the baskets in for self service by Saturday, I'll take you to the Michigan-Michigan State football game." So we went down to the Bradley Wholesale Grocery Company in Greenville and got the baskets. I think they cost us about 10 cents apiece, or a dollar a dozen for a double-handled market basket. I think we got two dozen of those baskets. We built a little corral, maybe four feet square, unnested the baskets, dumped them in loosely, and put a sign up "take a basket, help yourself." Well, I came home from the football game that night, and my dad says, "You know what happened?"

"No." I don't think I'd had a chance to look over the baskets.

"Well, you know that sign you made that said, 'Take a basket, help yourself?' The people did. The baskets are all gone. They didn't serve themselves to groceries and return the basket to the counter. They helped themselves to the baskets."

WELFARE ORDERS

When the welfare came into being, we accepted welfare orders. As a matter of fact we at one time did 60 percent of all the welfare business in Montcalm County--and there were 23 stores when we started in Greenville alone, plus the stores in Carson City, Howard City, Stanton, Sheridan, Sydney and many others in Montcalm County. But we in our store did 60 percent of all the welfare business in the whole county, and we were proud of that because we must have given value, and also treated people with dignity.

When we went into the taking of these welfare orders, Mr. Ranney said, "Don't you take those welfare orders. The country is going to go bankrupt. The country is now $35 billion in debt (that was in 1935) and the debt's as high as it can be and you're going to lose your welfare money that you have coming." But even though we had that warning, we continued to take in welfare orders, and we did an awful lot of business with welfare customers.

"Rock bottom prices every day" is the promise of this ad for the *"Thrift Self-Service Super Market,"* August 10, 1939

Preserve Dignity in every situation

BUYING BY OBJECTIVE

The independent grocery stores were getting a quarter a gallon or so for vinegar. A&P ran vinegar for 17 cents a gallon, and we had heard that a man named Mr. VanMaldegen in northwest Grand Rapids had a bunch of vinegar. He had too much for any merchant to buy. So he had the vinegar, and he was stuck with it. We'd heard about it from a Mr. Stanton over in Standale.

So my dad and I went there and my dad said, "Mr. VanMaldegen, I'd like to buy vinegar, and I'd like to buy it for 9 cents a gallon. Mr. VanMaldegen said, "That's what's the matter with you God-damn merchants. You want to buy it from me for 9 cents a gallon, and you don't care how much money I lose on it and you'll sell it for a quarter a gallon and make a lot of money on it, and you haven't any heart." He really bawled my dad out.

My dad left me standing there with Mr. VanMaldegen, and he turned around and walked out the door, slammed the door of the cider mill that we were standing in--and then opened it and came back in. By that time, Mr. VanMaldegen and I were both wondering what was going on when my dad said, "Mr. VanMaldegen, may I start over?" Well, how can you be mad at a man that's doing that? And Mr. VanMaldegen looked kind of odd and said, "Yes, start over," or something like that.

My dad said, "Mr. VanMaldegen, I know the retail merchants get 25 cents a gallon for vinegar, and I know that A&P gets 17 cents for vinegar. What I would like to do if possible-- and if it's not possible, tell me--I would like to buy a truckload of your vinegar, I'd like to take it to Greenville and sell it for 10 cents a gallon."

And Mr. VanMaldegen said, "If you will take it to Greenville and sell it for 10 cents a gallon, I would be happy to sell it to you for 9 cents a gallon." All we would gross on it, for all our work of coming to Grand Rapids, wrestling those big barrels and pumping it would be 50 cents a barrel, or $5. So we would really be losing our shirt selling his vinegar, but the moral of the story is, if you can make the seller understand your objective and ask him to be party to that objective, he will get emotionally involved and help you meet that objective at least some of the time. Well, we probably bought him out on vinegar.

CHAPTER 3
~
THE 40s

PEARL HARBOR DAY

On December 7, 1941 I was lying on my stomach in the living room. It was a nice warm day in December. The sun was coming in the plate glass windows that my dad had put into the house and I was listening to classical or semi-classsical music. I always liked Sigmund Romberg. I like opera too, but I like light opera better, and I was listening to music on my 22nd birthday when the news came. My dad was reading the paper. My sister may have been playing the violin. She was teaching in Mount Pleasant in those days. And we got the news that the Japanese had bombed Pearl Harbor.

TRYING TO ENLIST

Before we bought the Cedar Springs building, my dad wanted to know whether or not I was going to have to go in the Army. If I had to go in the Army, he wouldn't have bought the Cedar Springs building. In those days--this was prior to World War II--we were told that if we would enlist for a year, we'd get our service behind us and then we could go on about our business and not be wondering when we're going to get drafted. I tried the Army, the Air Force, and the Navy, and they all rejected me because I had a small hernia. I did wear a truss but didn't need one too badly. Every time they rejected me.

I was called up by the draft many times. I got to know the ropes so well going to Detroit they made me the leader of the bus.

One time they said, "You're in." They couldn't find my hernia so I called up my dad. I said, "This time I'm in," but then they sent me to a special review board. We lined up for this doctor, all bare naked. He never even looked up. He looked at my past record of coming down there, and he says you're out, and about 15 minutes later I called my dad. I says, "Well, I'm out."

I was in and out of the Army, and I never did get sworn in officially. There were times they took in people for limited service, and had I been there just at that time, I would have been in. They wouldn't allow you to enlist for limited service, they would only draft you and so I just had to float with events. It was kind of an odd feeling not to be in the Army because most of us felt very keenly that it was a war that had to be won.

A special section on Greenville in a Grand Rapids newspaper featured Fred and Hendrik (top right) among the town's "leading personalities." The date: December 7, 1941, the Sunday of the Japanese surprise attack on Pearl Harbor

PARTNERS, 1939

After having worked really full time all through high school--after school, nights, and Saturdays, Sundays, holidays and so forth--I liked the business. I had a lot of fun. I was needed. I don't remember much discussion about whether I should go to college because I think I liked being in the store and my folks wanted me there. I didn't feel put out because I couldn't go to college, although I've always been jealous of people who did, because I think I would have liked that too. But that was my choice.

Well, my dad said, "Hey, if you like this and you want to stay with it, I'll make you a full partner." Actually he was saying, "Okay, you're a full partner." We didn't have any incorporation papers. So now I'm a partner.

THE FIRST TRUCK

Our first truck was a pickup we hauled cattle in. During the war we hauled groceries and cattle and produce. We had a rack on top when we had the box full of groceries, in order to haul the produce on top of the truck. Of course, sometimes the produce dried out. But we hauled many a load of cattle.

CHICKENS & RATIONING

We had a slaughterhouse for quite awhile, and it helped a lot during the war. When we could not buy cattle one way, we could buy them live and slaughter them, and so we ended up trucking a lot of cattle. We were buying pigs in the market in Wayland and Ravenna, Owosso and St. Johns and Ionia, and in Rockford and a few other places. We also went clear over to near Owosso and bought chickens, because chickens, I think, were ration-free.

I can remember one time this Mrs. Rufus Johnson was in the store. She said, "I get so sick of chicken, chicken, chicken," and this other customer looked at Mrs. Johnson and said, "Oh, I get so sick of bologna, bologna, bologna; chicken would be heaven."

Wartime meant rationing of scarce commodities—a challenge for grocers but also an excuse for Meijer's Thrift Super Market to proclaim "there is no rationing on the savings we offer" in this advertisement from 1943

NEW SHOES

We ended up during the war time with ration stamps, and that was a real problem. We had stamps for sugar and stamps for shoes. Of course, we did not sell shoes then. But Lena tells the story how during the war she bought herself a pair of saddle shoes with only shoe ration coupons and she spilled India ink that we used on the stamp pads on those new shoes, and ruined their looks. She had worn them only about a day.

THE FEVER

Nineteen Forty is probably when we caught the fever to start another store--when we went to Kansas City to the Super Market Institute, and in '41 when we went with L.V. Eberhard to a meeting in Philadelphia. We were looking around here and there and all over. We looked at Fremont, we looked at Cedar Springs, at Hastings, Owosso, St. Johns.

At some point we landed on Cedar Springs, but before we went into it my dad did something similar to when we went into the "Thrifty Acres" concept, putting me on the spot: "Do you want it or don't you?"

He said to me, "You know Johanna is teaching in Mount Pleasant. You seem to like the business. I don't need a second store unless you want to stay with it."

JOHANNA IN CEDAR SPRINGS

My dad said, "Why don't we ask Johanna to come back and run the store in Cedar Springs?" She always seemed to enjoy the stores. And then he said, "Why don't we cut her in as a third partner?" So my dad approached Johanna and said, "Would you quit teaching and come back?" We opened the Cedar Springs store in '42.

During the war, there was very little male help. For four years Johanna was running the Cedar Springs store and worked very hard doing a lot of physical labor. As I recall, she had almost no manpower. She had men in the meat department; I think she had a man in produce, but she ran the rest of the store with part-timers. We took in hundreds of cases of eggs a week from the farmers. We would truck them around to wherever we could get the best price.

I remember the opening ad we had. One item was grapes, two pounds for 19. Kroger was across the street with grapes, two pounds for 19. Kroger was in a small store a block to the north when they took over a double building across the street and got open before we did. That really made us shake in our boots. And then we advertised grapes two pounds for 17 when Kroger was two pounds for 19. Kroger dropped the price to two for 15. We dropped the price to two for 15, Kroger dropped the price to five cents a pound. They were trying

The second Meijer store opened in 1942 in Cedar Springs, Michigan and was managed by Johanna (left), shown here with a young customer in one of the earliest versions of the shopping cart

their best to keep us from getting started, which I guess you can't blame them for, but then they asked us if we wanted to cooperate on similar store hours and my dad said, "You know the cooperation you gave us on grapes? That's the same cooperation you can expect from us on store hours." I think we always had longer store hours than Kroger. In addition, we never did drop our grape price to a nickel a pound. We stayed at two pounds for 15.

LOCKUP

We had a truck driver by the name of Fred Bond who later on became warehouse manager. A very nice fellow and a very hot-headed fellow. He was in the old Greenville store, and he would clerk in the store and drive truck when truck driving was needed. We gave him the keys to the store on Saturday night to lock the front door--for example, if we closed at 11:00 or 10:30 or something--years ago on Saturday nights we were open until after the movie got out because the farmers that came to town couldn't buy their perishables and then go to the movies so we'd stay open so the farmers could shop after the movie was out.

One night--well, two or three different Saturday nights, my dad would toss Fred Bond--or "Bondie" as we called him--the keys and Bondie would lock the door. Well, quite often somebody would come to the door just as you're locking it, and if my dad or my mother or I or maybe Lena were locking the door, we'd let that last customer in, but Bondie wouldn't. We closed, and he would shut the door. One night a guy was pounding on the door, and Bondie wouldn't let him in even though he was hollering, "My wife's in the store!"

BURIED INVENTORY

We did things in that old warehouse that you wouldn't be legally allowed to do today from a safety standpoint. We had to climb over the merchandise because we didn't have any aisles left. The aisles were full of merchandise.

In our effort to buy better and buy direct we would over-buy, and our back rooms were so full that we might have three cases of Broadcast Corn Beef Hash, but we'd have to order another case from the wholesale house in order to have it on the shelf because we couldn't get at the stuff that was buried in the back room.

If it must be done -
Do it + get it behind you.

The expanded Greenville store featured five checkouts in these 1943 photos. Above, with Hendrik (left), Fred, Al Waldorf and Dorothy Knight in the background, Lena Rader (left) and Mary Mulick run cash registers. Below, Hendrik stands between Gezina (far left) and Phyllis Kraft, with Lena Rader under the Muller bread sign at right.

LENA

About Lena...I had to review this with her first....You see, Lena and I have been married 95 years together if you add them both up. She was making $13 a week; she started at $12 the first of April in 1941 and she got a raise to $13. Then she got an offer from a hardware store, Greenville Hardware, for a $2 raise because a friend of hers worked there and told her employer about attributes that I did not appreciate I guess. So I went to my dad and said, "Well, Lena's going to leave."

My dad said, "We do not want that."

I said, "Well, nothing we can do about it. We cannot pay her $2 more."

"Maybe we ought to."

I said, "But you cannot pay her $2 more unless we pay the other five cashiers $2 more and that is six cashiers. That is $12 a week."

"Well," my dad said, "Maybe we ought to do that."

I said, "She isn't worth it."

At any rate, my dad thought we should raise all the cashiers and we did pay her $2 a week more. She didn't go to the hardware store. Five years later we started going together and now we are married. So if it was a good thing that we were married, then she lucked out. If it was bad, she should have gone to the hardware store.

WHERE'S THE FIRE?

Lena drove the truck out to the fire, and she was going pretty fast. It was the biggest truck we had, a big dual wheel two-ton, and the policeman pulled her over, and said, "Where do you think you're going, to a fire?" She says, "Yeah, the slaughterhouse is on fire."

BOOKKEEPING

When Lena started to work on the books as well as being a cashier and the other things that she did, we had all the invoices on the wall. If we had 50 suppliers, we had 50 nails. If we owed a bill we put it on the nail and when we paid the bill we took it off the nail and threw it away, and there is no way

Mr. and Mrs. George Rader
request the pleasure of your company
at the marriage of their daughter

Lena Elizabeth

to

Mr. Fred Meijer

on Saturday, January the fifth
nineteen hundred forty-six

at eight o'clock
at their home

Amble, Michigan

*Fred married Lena Rader
in the bride's home near
Lakeview, Michigan,
January 5, 1946*

we could reconstruct anything once we paid. The debt was all on the wall with the nails and the bills.

So we gave Lena a bushel basket full. We thought that anybody who was a cashier in a bank, who took bookkeeping in high school, could keep books, because my dad and I knew nothing and she knew something. She got to be a real good bookkeeper when we got accounting help and so forth over the years.

THE FIRE

Lena and I were married January 5, 1946 and a few months later the Greenville store burned. We were living on Van Deinse Avenue in a remodeled house, and the firemen rapped on the window and had us come down there. The whole store was one sea of flames.

We could see the cash register sitting there, but no way you could get at it. The store was just about a total loss. We lost an awful lot of money relative to our net worth in that Greenville fire. We had complete coverage on the merchandise, which saved us, but we only had $5,000 coverage on the building and $5,000 insurance coverage on the fixtures, and I think the new Quonset we put up cost $40,000 for the building and about $40,000 for the fixtures, so you can see we were really strapped for cash. But it was lucky that we had the merchandise so well covered by insurance. We didn't have business interruption insurance. That would have been better yet. But it was enough to save us from going bankrupt. This was in, I think, March or April in 1946 that the store burned, and the Ionia store opened in August of '46 so instead of almost having three stores, we went to one store, and that was Cedar Springs only, during the summer of 1946.

About the time our first store burned down, we were looking for a man named John Watson, who we had heard was a dealer in Quonset buildings. At the same time, there was a man named Bill George who had a Quonset on a truck in Newaygo, which he ordered for somebody without a good contract. The person didn't want it, and he was stuck with the Quonset.

Coincidentally this all happened the same time as our fire. Also, we had acquired a site a block south and across the street for a new store.

So we were looking for a Quonset when Bill George calls up. He's got a Quonset and he was just a godsend. So anyway, by the time night fell--the store burned maybe at four o'clock in the morning--the smoke was still smoldering when we had the building delivered to a new site. Mr. Matt Heyn, who was president of the Grand Rapids Wholesale Grocery Company, came up to give us his condolences and see the fire. My dad

Fire destroyed the much-expanded original Meijer store in Greenville, May 1946. In what was one of the worst fires in the town's history, Fred remembers how the cereals ignited, while the densely packed paper products were slow to burn

took him across the street to show him where the new store was going to be built, and Mr. Heyn said, "Henry, don't look so happy. People will think you burned it down."

And my dad says, "My gosh, we lost pretty near the whole building, had almost no insurance on the building, almost no insurance on the fixtures. We did have good insurance on the merchandise, and you want me to be sad so people won't think I burned it down? Nuts to them. I'm not going to go around crying and putting on a long face just so people won't think I burned the store down."

TREES

Later on after this fire we were talking about and when we built the Quonset a block south across the street, there were some beautiful trees on the street, but we desperately needed that street widened. We didn't know what to do because we knew if we told everybody about it, there would be a groundswell to save those beautiful trees, and really we could not blame them for saving those trees.

On the other hand, you couldn't get the traffic down the main street. The street would have been widened sooner or later anyway, but we needed it widened quickly, and we wanted to widen our side so that the people could get to our store. So we got permission from the city manager to cut the trees down, and the minute we got permission--or not the minute but let's say we got it on Wednesday afternoon, then Thursday about four o'clock in the morning we sent some-body in to cut all those trees down. By the time the people went to work, the trees were all down. If we'd have cut them down one tree at a time, we'd have been held up for months. It really worked out fine.

I guess it was ethical. We didn't wait to get a lot of static, and we ended up widening the street, which was very good for the neighborhood, and it was very good for our store.

This Quonset structure, erected to replace the burned-out store across Lafayette Street, opened in the summer of 1946

UNLOADING CEMENT

Once, in Ionia, we tried to buy cement as cheap as we could. A semi came up with a load of cement that we had purchased direct, but then the driver said, "It's not my job to unload." So my dad had to unload all the cement. He had to haul the cement by hand about 60 feet because he didn't have a wheelbarrow or conveyor, and put it in a garage that we had. And so he called me up and said, "I need some help in unloading this truck." I brought another fellow along with myself to Ionia, and here was my dad stripped down to his waist and hauling this cement. He had the trailer unloaded, and he was unloading the semi-truck part. It was a truck and a trailer. He was sweating profusely and working his heart out--enjoying it.

That would be about 1945 so he was already 61 years old, and the chief of police came by and said, "Henry Meijer, you're going to have a heart attack." It was almost a wonder he didn't because he worked so hard. But he was pretty used to hard work over his life--hard physical work going way back to the foundry days--and he kept himself in pretty good shape. So we helped him unload the last quarter or third of the load, and we got her off.

Also, we tried to buy cement blocks as cheaply as we could. We started out years before when we had additions to put on, buying used blocks and cleaning them up. Then we bought sand lime blocks. We got them from near the corner of Boston and Kalamazoo Street in Grand Rapids and then later on we bought cement blocks and haydite blocks and waylite blocks. They were lighter and made out of a kind of cinder material that had better insulation qualities, but we would haul these with the same truck we hauled groceries with, and then when we got to Ionia we had to unload them. We didn't have any conveyors. My dad and I would unload them. When we laid the blocks to build the store, they called us the slave labor because we hired professional block layers, but they didn't handle the blocks, and so my dad would pitch them up to the first level on the scaffold to me and then I would pitch them up to the next level on the scaffold to where they were laying up the wall, and that's the way we got the job done.

We tried to save electricity by putting in sky lights in Ionia, but like in Cedar Springs, they weren't that practical and over the years, we enclosed them. I remember debating at length with ourselves as to whether we should put in two-tube or four-tube fixtures that would double our lighting cost. We went for the bigger fixture, which worked out very well. The store was quite large for those days, 12,000 square feet with a graveled parking lot. Johanna and Don worked there during the opening. Don Magoon came to work for the company, I think, just prior to opening the Ionia store. Don spent most of his time during the opening days pushing cars out that got stuck in the parking lot.

Meijer first employed its familiar "Why Pay More" slogan—punctuated by a question mark that later gave way to an exclamation point—with the opening of the Ionia store in 1946. Fred and Hendrik frequently visited stores together, as in this photo in the Ionia parking lot, c. 1949

BUYING A WAREHOUSE AT BANKRUPTCY

We needed some warehouse space and Metzger went bankrupt in Greenville. His wooden warehouse was going to be sold--that's on North Lafayette Street at Congress Street, right near the tracks. It was going to be sold along with a lot of other potato warehouses. I think they were in Entrican and Edmore, and there were maybe a dozen of them. I don't know how many potato warehouses. Well, anyway, it was up for bid in the bankruptcy court and we put in our bid, and we went the day--let's say, for example, it was 2:00 in the afternoon that we were supposed to be there on a certain Friday, and the bids were supposed to be opened. Well, we walked in at maybe 5 minutes after 2:00, if that was the time, and the referee in bankruptcy came running out and he said, "Oh, are you Mr. Boss? We've been waiting for you."

My dad says, "No, I'm Henry Meijer; I bid on the building."

"Oh, we were looking for Mr. Boss."

"Oh."

"Well what are you looking for him for?"

"He's coming in yet with a bid."

"He's coming in with a bid," my dad said, "and it's just after 2:00, and the bids are supposed to be closed at 2:00 and opened so we know who won! What kind of a crooked outfit is this? And you mean this is run by the government? A crooked deal like this?"

"Well," he says, "you can put in a bid on the whole thing if you want to."

My dad says, "Okay, I'll put in a bid for the whole thing," and we put in a modest bid for the whole thing. "Well," he says, "you're out, there's a higher bid." And my dad says, "You're damn right I knew I was out. If it's going to be an auction sale, why didn't you tell us? I thought at least the federal government was honest about this thing, but if they're as crooked as that, there's no chance for anybody."

Well, anyway, Boss came in with his bid, as I recall it, about 3 or 4 o'clock in the afternoon. My dad and I were somewhere else and I said, "Let's call back and see who got the building," because the man in the bankruptcy court told us to call back later on that afternoon, and they'd tell us who it was. My dad was so disgusted and mad that he wouldn't call back because

This vacant potato warehouse became the small chain's first office and ware-house in 1946. Below, Fred and Lena (far right) join Hendrik (third from left) and other associates in front of the company's first tractor-trailer

he said it's a crooked outfit and we'll never get it.

I says, "Gee, dad, it won't hurt us to make a telephone call," and my dad said, kind of mad and pouting, "You call if you want to, I'm not going to waste my time on it."

I'm going to do it. I called, and the man said, "You got the building." And then we put together what we think happened. Now we can't be sure of this, but we think it happened like this: That Tom Metzger was waiting in an office in the building there, and he had a right to see all the bids that came in, and so the minute he saw all the bids that came in, we think, then he called Hugh Boss and said, for example if the bids for all the buildings together were $28,000, "You bid $29,000 and we'll get the whole thing back," and I think they were all in cahoots to put it into bankruptcy and then bid it back. Then Hugh would come in, and this would all happen in a matter of minutes--just top the bids and take the buildings all back. Well, we just happened to walk in at the right time or the wrong time, and I think the bankruptcy court man was honest, but he was being used and didn't know the timing and what was going on. And maybe Metzger was working with his lawyers on just how to do this, I don't know, so it's maybe at five minutes to 2:00 you'll see all the bids and at two minutes after 2:00 or just 2:00 the man comes in with a higher bid that he calls and then by quarter after 2:00, he's got all the buildings back.

Well, anyway, I think because my dad lost his temper and called the court all the names he did--well, he didn't call them a lot of names, but he made it very emphatic and we could have sued the court to have it overturned had we known, but we would never have done it because we wouldn't have known that much. My dad would have never gone to court for it, but that's how we got that wooden warehouse building. If we hadn't walked in at that moment, I think it would have gone some other way, and it would have gone through bankruptcy and the people who put it through bankruptcy would have wiped out their debts and gotten all their buildings back. But we just happened to throw a wrench into the deal and it was purely accidental. That building worked out fine until we moved to Grand Rapids.

Among the returning servicemen making 1946 a popular year for weddings was Army Captain Don Magoon (right), who married Johanna Meijer with newlyweds Fred and Lena in attendance

FROM A LETTER TO HENDRIK
TUESDAY, JUNE 1

Don really enjoyed the meetings [Super Market Institute], *he came home almost ready to start a new store, like we always used to do. Those supermarket operators sure believe in going ahead.*

EXPANDING

We bought the property in Ionia in '45. My dad figured that when the war was over, there would be a lot of men looking for work, and the site had a valley with a creek in it that had to be tiled and a hill. He would have a group of men work with wheelbarrows and fill this valley and level it off so we could have the store and the parking lot. But that was the most impractical idea.

We often got into situations that were very impractical, but we got into them. We had to get out of them, and we ended up getting out in a very practical way and seeing the project through. Before we got done, we had cranes, we had bulldozers, we had dump trucks and we had all kinds of equipment in there. A far cry from just wheeling all that dirt around with wheelbarrows, which we first intended to do.

WAY TOO BIG

When we opened the Ionia store, we had a visit from Bill Albers, who had a bunch of supermarkets in Cincinnati, Ohio. He was the ex-president of Kroger and had started his own chain of supermarkets after he left Kroger. He came up with his brother, who was Bishop Albers in Lansing, and he told us our store was way too big. For years we thought it was too big, too. He was right. It was 12,000 square feet though, and by today's standards it looks very small. And the next time we built a store, which was on South Division in Grand Rapids, we built a 10,000-foot store which was a little more sensible size supermarket for those days. On the other hand, over the years, we enlarged that South Division store to 15,000 feet and then 20,000 feet and we enlarged the Ionia store later on to 17,000 feet, so you can see how things change.

SOMETHING FOR POOR PEOPLE

When we would run ads, and we would run something fancy, my dad always wanted to know, what type of merchandise did we have for the poor people? He could so well remember his early days in the Netherlands when they needed the cheapest meat and the cheapest beans and the cheapest

*On a snapshot of the Greenville store he sent to Hendrik in Europe, Fred
describes the informal way a decision was reached when the facade was
painted in 1948*

peas and the cheapest bread, and he always wanted to know,
what are we doing for the poor people? What are we doing for
people that can't afford these fancy foods? That always stuck
in my mind.

HOW YOU TREATED MY PARENTS

The South Division store finally opened in 1949. That was our first store with automatic front doors, Magic Eye front doors. We really thought we had the latest, which it was in those days, as well as radiant heat in the floor and everything else.

One of the first customers we had was a lady I went to school with, and she says to us, "You know why I trade in this store?" She was from Greenville and we thought, well, maybe because we knew her in Greenville, and maybe we had the finest store in town or maybe because of automatic doors or low prices or a new building, but her answer was, "I'm trading here because you were so nice to my parents when we were on the welfare in Greenville." It just gives another indication how people, if you treat them decently, value that more than anything else.

FROM A LETTER TO HENDRIK
MONDAY, MAY 24, 1948

Elmer, the produce man, sent some geraniums to Ionia Saturday. Lloyd called him at Cedar to say he did not want them. Then after Elmer told him to take them he sent them back to Greenville anyway. I had been in Ionia when they opened at 7:30 a.m. Saturday and was just back when Elmer reported this to me. I really got mad and went to Ionia again Saturday afternoon. I took Lloyd, Bill Weed and Elmer all up in the little office and we had it out. I wanted Bill Weed and Elmer in on it so Lloyd could not grumble afterwards and misquote me. I went over all the things I had been wanting to say for some time plus the flower deal. He took it like a fish and I think the air is clear now and we will get good cooperation in the future. This is the first time he has ever been criticized by us and I guess he needed it. I am glad it happened but when I started I did not know whether he would take it or quit.

From Ionia I went to Cedar Springs, I wanted to trip up Harold Lehman if I could. I gave him some produce price changes Friday morning and when I checked him Saturday he had only changed two of the four items. This is the first time I have had a chance to trip him up myself; before, Elmer always gave him the changes. I called Harold to one side and asked him if he thought I was kidding when I gave him changes. I think we understand each other now if he did not before.

Fred (left) and Hendrik present a lucky customer with a basketload of groceries during the grand opening of the first Grand Rapids supermarket in 1949

My Father set the tone
I guess I also help set the tone

GRAND RAPIDS

It dawned on us that everything in Western Michigan starts and stops in Grand Rapids. Wholesalers of all kinds are there. We finally saw that it was the closest metropolitan area and the biggest. So in '48 we decided we were going to go to Grand Rapids. We tried several locations. We tried to get the location that is now a Perry drugstore on Plainfield Avenue, but that was destined to go to an A&P store. And then we heard about a store on Eastern Avenue, but it had been taken. We were still looking and we found the site at 4242 South Division, which is also a Perry drugstore now. We bought that property and we opened that in the spring of '49. Well in the meantime the Eastern Avenue store became available because someone else's deal failed and they came to us and said "Do you still want it?" We worked out a deal and in the spring we opened South Division, and late summer or fall we opened Eastern, so we went from three stores to five.

It was a big, big jump. At the same time, the other change was that when we were only in Greenville, nobody carried the key but the family—my sister was in Cedar Springs, she carried the key there. When we went to Ionia, and at the same time my sister had gotten married and gotten pregnant, we went from two stores where family carried all the keys to three stores which needed managers, that was one of the big milestones. And then you go to five stores—then you have to start developing management principles.

work up objectives together,
rather than give orders

CHAPTER 4
~
THE 50s

FROM AN INTERVIEW IN *SUPERMARKET NEWS,*
JUNE 16, 1952

Our function is to perform a public service, and the better job we do of rendering a service, the greater will be the demand for our service.

It may sound strange, but one of the worst worries is that people do not complain enough. We welcome complaints because they help us improve our service.

We also know that many customers who may have a reason to complain or make suggestions as to how we can better serve them, never do so. We believe that if we can get customers to tell us what we have done that displeased them or what we can do better to satisfy them, we can improve our service and keep them as a customer. It is the customer who does not complain and does not come back that we would like to reach and talk with. Maybe they can help us, maybe we can help them. We must keep that relationship between us and our customers open and continuing by making them understand we are trying to serve and satisfy.

Our aim is to gain their confidence and demonstrate that most of all we want to satisfy them. If possible, we never let a customer leave our store unhappy or leave a customer unhappy in their home.

We try to get across to our employees the idea they are not to uphold our practices and defend us if our policies and practices fall short of giving the customer everything she has a right to expect; or to make the customer feel embarrassed or apologetic in making a complaint.

admit when you're wrong

Lena helped with
bookkeeping and
advertising layout
until her first child
was born in 1952

Checkout lines stretch down the aisles at the opening of Store #6, Michigan
Street and Fuller Avenue in Grand Rapids, in February 1952

BABIES AND ADVERTISING

Lena was pregnant with our first child as we approached the opening of Fuller, and we had an advertising manager that did other things, too, Maxine Barton, a very good employee. When she quit suddenly, Maxine, who was working on the grand opening ads, just left us with the ads.

Because Lena and I had done the advertising layouts and drafting and so forth so many years, I took all the advertising home and said to Lena, "You and I have to work out the grand opening ads." We were going to have an insert in the Grand Rapids Herald as our big grand opening splash, and so Lena was working on the insert and I was working on the Grand Rapids Press ad, and she was heavy as the dickens and over-due with the baby when the doctor calls up, and says, "We've decided to take your baby Caesarean. Be at the hospital at four o'clock this afternoon so that we can deliver the baby tomor-row morning."

Well, that really didn't go over so well. Lena burst out in tears, and the water was dripping down on the ad paper. I saw that wasn't going to work, so I took all the ads back to the office, and I think we had a supervisor named Jack Van Overloop out of that first store, and I says, "Jack, here, you do the ads, you finish them, here's what we had in mind. I got to take Lena to the hospital."

When our baby (Hank) was born, because all the salesmen were helping to stock the new store and the contractors were finishing the building, her room was just full of flowers. Never afterwards did she ever get that many flowers, just because of the timing. And I can remember my dad being so excited and several people calling up and saying, "Hey, you know, this isn't so bad. A lot of people have had Caesarean. I've had it or my mother's had it or my sister or my wife or somebody," and all trying to reassure her that it wasn't that tough a problem. It worked out fine, and our other two children were born the same way.

Children aren't our property they don't owe us anything

Fred cuts and pastes an advertising layout at home, c. 1952

Lena holds son Doug soon after his birth in January 1954

A BANKER IS NEVER WRONG

We had built the South Division store with a $25,000 mortgage from the Old Kent Bank, and the Eastern Store building was rented, which was our first rental experience, so we didn't have to get money to build the building, but we did need money to put in the fixtures and the merchandise.

So we went to the Old Kent Bank to raise our mortgage on South Division from $25,000 to $35,000, which they did, were happy to do, apparently. We went to Greenville to borrow money to put in the inventory of the Eastern Store, and they had us sign a chattel mortgage to secure themselves.

Well, I didn't know how dangerous a chattel mortgage is to your credit. We did get a pledge from them not to record the chattel mortgage, but they did record it, and the minute they recorded it, we could no longer get deliveries from a lot of companies because they weren't going to sell to anybody who had a chattel mortgage on their merchandise. That was a real lesson to us because no way in the future, no matter how badly we needed money, would we ever dare put a chattel mortgage on our merchandise--a lien on our merchandise-- and we never did do it again, either.

Anyway, the Old Kent Bank had agreed, prior to our starting the Fuller Store, to loan us $125,000 as a mortgage against the building we were going to build at Fuller and Michigan, and the building was supposed to house the warehouse in the basement, the store on the main floor and, in addition to the store on the main floor, the offices up behind.

When the Korean War came along, and we didn't have our foundations in legally to build the supermarket, we did have the legal right to build an office and a warehouse. That was permitted, so we proceeded on the basis that the whole building was an office and warehouse, knowing we couldn't open the store and would have to use it all for an office and warehouse until such time as it became legal to open the store.

The bank became apprehensive because we couldn't put in the supermarket, which, hopefully, would be profitable and would be important to our paying off our debts to them. They mentioned that all office expense and all warehouse expense is always overhead. But if it's necessary, it's necessary overhead. We dealt with a man named Martin Lilly, a vice president of

The store on S. Division Avenue (above) and one on Eastern Avenue
(below) marked the small chain's entry into Grand Rapids in 1949

the Old Kent Bank, and Mr. Lilly said you have to see Mr. Heber Curtis. Mr. Curtis was an old-style banker, and we talked to him at the same time he was having problems loaning money to Ben Duthler and to L.V. Eberhard, and he says, "You grocers are all alike. You get in over your head and expect the bank to help you out."

We tried to explain to him that we made the deal with them, and they should stick with it. And he says, "Well, you can't put in a supermarket now and that's not our fault. We're only going to loan you $75,000." That was $50,000 less than we expected. Mr. Curtis continued to say, "You merchants always spend more than you expect, and you always make the bank bail you out."

I said, "Mr. Curtis, we have never in our life done that. When we make a deal, we try to think it through well enough so we don't have to come back, and we've never come back to the bank for more money to complete a deal. When we've made a mistake, we've figured out a way to complete the project without going back to the bank."

He says, "You did it on South Division. You didn't have enough money, and you borrowed $25,000 and then you came back for 10 more."

I said, "Mr. Curtis, that's not true. We borrowed that money to open the Eastern store. We borrowed $25,000 to open Division, and we opened it. And then we came to you and said we would like to open the Eastern Store, would you help us finance that by putting in an additional $10,000 and taking additional mortgage on the South Division store, which was well worth the money."

He proceeded to tell me that's not the way he remembered it, and I suppose I was a pretty young kid to be talking back to the banker that way. But to make my point more complete, I went back to the office, documented every one of our moves and wrote him a letter explaining that I was right.

Well, I found out you can be ever so right with a stubborn banker, but you aren't going to get your money. So I was right, but I was dumb.

*A poor substitute for one of Fred's favorite pastimes was this oil drum at a
dude ranch in northern Michigan c. 1951*

DELEGATING

Actually my dad was marvelous at delegating everything to
me, and I think it helped me to do the job. With that example
and the atmosphere that I worked in I always delegated pretty
nearly everything. And I think it has helped me be a better
manager. It's helped people like Harvey and Earl to develop,
rather than hovering over detail--allowing them to do their
own thing. The one thing that my dad always believed in was
treating everyone with dignity. I mean, he was obsessed with
that. He would fail, and make mistakes, and he'd blow up
sometimes. And he would tell me story after story about his
Army experiences, about treating people with dignity, about
how the captain, after putting him in the guardhouse for being
AWOL, made him a corporal.

When you have good people, you've got to let them do their

thing, make mistakes and be human. Basically the people who don't always adhere to every rule are the people who sometimes help you change the rules that ought to be changed. My dad made mistakes, but he believed in not bawling out people. If they made a mistake he wanted to help them to succeed. Basically he did that with me.

As we grew, you had to delegate, and you had to reorganize your responsibilities. I remember one particular incident when Harvey Lemmen was operations man. As a matter of fact, going back one step, Harvey came in as an accountant, an office manager, in our first main office. We had five or six stores by the time he came to work for us, and he came from the University of Michigan as an honors student, graduated with an accounting degree.

We never thought of him in any other position but accounting and office management. Well, we went into our own warehousing. We hired some experts after we were in for awhile, and they showed us how to lay out the warehouse so that we would use less aisle space and we could use straddle fork trucks and so forth. We turned the aisles from, let's say east to west to north to south, and we lost track of where all the merchandise was. We had a warehouse manager named Pat Reynolds, and he threw up his hands in disgust and just walked out, and we never saw him again. He says, "These darned experts"--he probably used stronger words--"I can't run this warehouse the way they've got things all goofed up."

So over the years that'd be my job: to go in and try to run something that my dad didn't have time to do or all of us couldn't do. I used to get thrown into various jobs, and this was my job--to run the warehouse. I guess somebody had to run it. We didn't have any management to run it.

Then I thought to ask Harvey, "How would you like to run the warehouse?" He'd just gone from accountant to being controller, and really had just a week or so in that job, and hadn't had a chance to get started in it.

He said, "I don't know anything about warehousing."

I says, "Well, neither do I, but one of us has to do it and you've got more time than I have. I'd like to have you do it if you will."

This former factory on Alpine Avenue in Grand Rapids served as the company's first Grand Rapids warehouse

"Well," he says, "I'll try, but I don't know anything about it."

So Harvey put on green dungarees. I just couldn't help but smile because I'd never seen him in anything but a suit and a tie, and he went in there and tried to run the warehouse. After a day or so, with everything in such a mess, all of us were over there trying to find things. We had four-wheeled trucks that we worked the orders on in those days, and I remember it took me one or two hours just to find the stuff to go on one four-wheeled truck, and we had everybody from the office over there just picking merchandise and pulling these trucks.

Harvey said, "These experts got us in trouble. Maybe they could help us get out of trouble. Do you mind if I call them up?"

And I said, "No, go ahead."

So Harvey calls up Philadelphia, this man came up on the next plane, in a half a day he was there, and by golly he knew how to straighten that warehouse out. Within a day or two the stuff was rolling normally. So Harvey's claim to fame as an operating man in the warehouse was that he knew enough to go for help when we needed it, and he did and got us out of trouble.

FROM LETTERS TO HENDRIK

THURSDAY, JUNE 14, 1956

I feel that if we change the name on the Downtown Store, the employees will still say, "Yes, we work for Meijer's." And if we raise the prices and they associate it with Meijer, it is liable to be bad advertising for our other stores because it will lead people to believe that our prices are higher in our other stores. Also, that even if we could put it in the black, that we are still piddling to monkey with it and we would be just as well off to concentrate on the nine good stores we have.

I cannot help but think that Milton Sage out in California closed up a $40,000 per week store, because he felt that it was too far out of his normal course of travel to supervise properly and he chose to close it up rather than to keep it.

I still cannot see making enough profit in these restaurants unless we do a really big beautiful job and then of course, it is a big gamble. I had dinner with Harvey Koning in the Humpty Dumpty restaurant on Leonard Street and they serve a very fine noonday lunch for 69 cents. It was tuna fish salad and several other items. It was a family operation and they are making good wages plus a little, but when we run them, somebody else makes the wages and they are not as conscientious and the operation is not big enough to have a really tiptop manager. I think we will have a hard time making a profit or let me say, we will probably operate at loss while some little family is operating a restaurant at a profit.

WEDNESDAY, JUNE 27, 1956

We just bought two singing commercials. One for Meijer's and one for the Good Will Stamp Company. They each cost about $200.00--they are real cute. We all just heard them a few minutes ago.

We had our meeting at Morton yesterday which is the second meeting we have had on financial statements for review and projection. I think those meetings are well worth while. Everyone seems to enjoy them and they all have a lot more of the facts of life concerning the business. I did not tell the people at the meeting what I had in mind or what I have been talking to you about the restaurant or

*Fred (right), Hendrik (left), Don Magoon and colleagues outside the
company's tiny store in downtown Grand Rapids in 1955*

about the Downtown store, but we did review the losses in the operation and during the meeting Pat Jameson suggested that we close up
the restaurant. We explored it a little further, I did not give them any
indication of my thinking, then I had them vote and they voted
100% to close up the restaurant rather than spending another
$8,000 on it. I did not say we would abide by their vote, and I asked
them to keep it confidential.

Then we got into the losses of the Downtown Store. I asked for a
vote on that and they voted six in favor of closing it and four in
favor of changing the name and raising the prices if that could be
worked out practically. I still think we should close both of them
myself, but I did not tell them that.

Ask for help its not a weakness

CONVENTION IN FLORIDA

On our first trip to Boca Raton, my dad and I came down on the train. It had to be before 1948. So we get into the train station. I do not know if the train was late or what. But we asked this truck driver, "How do you get from the train station to Boca Raton?" It is not too far, it was almost walking distance in the old days, but you do not walk with your baggage, and there was not any taxi there, and we just looked around, did not know quite what to make of it, and asked, "How do we get to Boca Raton?"

I think they probably offered to call a car, but I cannot remember now. "Why can't we ride with you?" we asked.

"Well, there's two of us and there's just this cab. We're just taking baggage."

"Well, can't we hop on the back of the truck?"

So, we hopped on the back of the truck. It was a stake truck, and my dad and I stood there hanging on to the side of the truck like we did on the farm or any place else, and we roll up to the front door of the very fancy Boca Raton hotel on the back of the truck, and as we're coming up to the door, here is L.V. Eberhard and his wife. We weren't embarrassed, we just had a good laugh.

MY DAD

He would always say, "You can do it." And he would help you to succeed, and now we're trying to teach our managers that the best thing they can do is to be the best helper to their managers. When people are working for them, to be their first assistants, to manage by objective, help the person reach the objective, help him or her learn all those little things that are so important to success on the job. All these things my dad practiced without any formal training. How he came to such an approach, I don't know, but he taught the approach or he knew the approach that is being taught in very sophisticated university classes today on management by objective.

When we would make a mistake, he used to say, "Well, you always have to pay for a college education," meaning you made a mistake, it cost you money; if you learned something, well, maybe the lesson was worth the cost.

Hendrik and Fred at the Bal Harbour Hotel in Boca Raton, Florida.
(The popular convention site was also the winter home of Grand
Rapids tycoon Frank McKay, notorious powerbroker in Michigan
Republican politics who once helped the Meijers arrange bank
financing and took out his fee in groceries)

Dad wasn't always right or fair but
he had the best of intentions

COLLEAGUES & KIDS

My father used to say getting to be a father is nothing, being one--that's something. That's really stuck in my mind over the years as a father. It's been hard to know when you're doing a right job.

I happen to believe very much in birth control, planned parenthood and the right of a woman to have an abortion. I don't believe in abortion as a way of birth control, but I think it's much better not to have a child born than to have an unloved child.

Being a parent is a long-time job. You never cease being a parent no matter how old you are, but for 20 years of your life between the time your first child is born and the time that last one is mature, you almost have to build your life around your children, and not feel imposed.

I don't feel employees owe their employer anything or employers owe employees anything. I think we should try to be good employers and do to other people like we'd want them to do to us if we were working for someone else. We do it for our own sake, wanting to be a good employer, and I think an employee should want to do a good job for his or her own sake.

I think it is the same with having children. Children basically don't owe their parents anything, and their parents--I suppose--don't owe their children anything except the children didn't ask to be born and, therefore, I think, the parents do owe the children a loving home life and a decent atmosphere in which to grow. If this isn't a joy to a person, then they shouldn't have children. It should be a joy to do. We've had a lot of fun with our family. As they grow older we miss some of those early years, except that you know you can't hang on to them forever, and you only hope that you've been a good parent, because you realize, like the song from "South Pacific" says, "you learn to hate by 7 or 8." By 7 or 8, children have established a lot of their lifelong patterns, and hopefully you've done a good enough job so that they can adjust to the world and end up having a satisfactory relationship with the world.

Each of our sons started working in the store at the age of 11 or 12, part time--doing something, earning a little something.

The Meijers and the Magoons

The family posed for this portrait in 1953

As we became a little more affluent, or had our names on all these buildings even though most of them were mortgaged, you questioned your own role as a parent. When do you provide too much, too little? What is a happy balance? One of my problems is, I never did know for sure, and I still don't know. I guess the only saving part of this is that probably nobody else knows either so we all go through life just doing the best we can.

I will say this, though. If your marriage works out fairly well, that's good, and it's also partly luck, and if your children come out to be decent human beings, that's all you can expect, and that's good. And that, too, I suppose, is partly luck. So, if we've been good parents, and that's why it is, that's good. If it's luck, that's good. Maybe there's a combination someplace.

GETTING INTO TOPCO

We knew a fellow named Wayne Brown in Columbus, Ohio, and we knew Mr. Steve Mugar who had the Star Markets in Boston, and several others, and we never thought we would get in to Topco but when we were big enough to get in we wanted in, and when they thought we might be big enough, man we just jumped at the chance.

Eberhard and Plumb said, "We'll buy together and so we'll make a pretty good member of Topco." So we went to work lobbying and we called up Syl Goldman, we called up Wayne Brown, we called up Steve Mugar.

As a matter of fact, every time I go to Washington, which isn't very often, I see the Washington Monument and out in front of the Washington Monument there's a telephone booth. I was on that phone one time for about an hour while the group that was with me at a controller's conference at the National Association of Food Chains was touring the monument. I was talking to these guys about getting into Topco. Well, what they ended up doing is they rejected us all (Meijer, Plumb, & Eberhard) and then after they rejected us all, they let a little time lapse, and then they said to us a couple months later, "Would you be willing to accept Plumb if you came into Topco?" We didn't want to, but we knew darn well if we didn't we might not get in, and I found out afterwards we would not have gotten in.

So, fine, yeah, we'd be glad to. Didn't mean a word of it, but they said, "Okay, if you're willing to have Plumb come in, too, because you fellahs need to buy together to get enough volume."

Syl Goldman thought well of us, and he was in our corner when we were lobbying. I know Wayne Brown was in our corner. He said "Eberhard's not our kind of guy. Meijer is. We want Meijer." That's how we got in.

"Then we'll accept you and Plumb." And we said okay. At that time, we had the same territory that Plumb did. We never did buy together. It didn't work out at all.

Meijer joined the Topco buying cooperative in 1955. Displaying some of the products soon to be featured in company supermarkets were (from left) Charles Magoon, Charles Hammett, Hendrik Meijer, Fred and Don Magoon

Fred (second row, fourth from right) joined Meijer store managers and other executives (including, top row, from left, Earl Holton and Harvey Lemmen) for a training seminar, c. 1957

IT'S THEM OR ME

Back in 1946, Greenville reopened just ahead of Ionia. We had a manager that we hired from Muskegon named Harold. Harold was a real nice man. He had failed as a manager for Plumb and was working in a shoe store, and we thought that he could be the manager of the Greenville store. Our labor was too high, and the stock was not getting on the shelf. We really had a problem because we had gaping holes on the shelf where we needed merchandise. He was just not getting the job done--even though he had basically the same old crew that we had before the fire.

I finally sent him home to Muskegon and ran the store myself for a couple of weeks because we just had to get the store in shape. I didn't feel right managing around him. I told him, "You take a week off, and then we'll talk after that."

So we got the store up in shape, and then I went to Muskegon to sit down and talk with him about his future with us and where we go from here. He said, "Well, my problem is I only hired one new person and that was Bob. All the rest of the people are loyal to you, and unless I can fire everybody in the store except Bob, I can't run that store."

And I said, "By golly, if we have to choose between losing the whole crew of old timers and losing you, that's no choice at all. I'm sorry, Harold, but we have to lose you because we aren't going to fire all these people that have been with us so long just so you got a crew that you hired."

Its your job to help others to succeed

Fred presents an award to meat manager Charles Bradley, c. 1956. Also on hand (from left) are long-time meat director Roland Van Valkenberg, manager Cal Rupers, retired deputy chairman Harvey Lemmen and buyer George Mikita

expect & work for the best

PROMOTIONS

In one promotion, or carnival, or whatever we called it, we had free peanuts that you could eat, and just throw the peanut shucks on the floor. And so customers threw them on the floor. But the tile floors were asphalt tile in those days. Peanut shells have a little oil in them, and after you walked on them a little while, you could take your fingernail and scoop up the floor tile. It took us a while to figure that out, and we quit that. It was an interesting promotion, but it practically wrecked all of our floors.

DON'T MEAN NOTHING TO ME

For the opening of the Fuller Store, we trained the cashiers and then the night before the opening, we had some meetings so that I could meet everybody and talk about our store policies. We still have that general plan, although we do it a little earlier now. And I had gone into the Eastern Avenue Store, giving out candy and cigars because our first son was born just a few days prior to the opening. There was a lady training at Eastern Avenue named Isabelle Czarnowski, and I said, "Would you like a cigar or candy?" Being facetious, thinking being a lady she would take the candy, which she did.

She says, "Thanks, so what's that for?"

I said, "We just had a baby boy."

She says, "Who are you?"

I says, "I'm Fred."

She says, "Don't mean nothing to me."

Well, that was just a few days before we opened, and the night before we opened, we had this store meeting. The store manager introduced me to the group and said, "Fred Meijer would like to say a word" and out of the crowd one lady's hand goes up in front of her face and she hollered, "Oh, no!" It was Isabelle, who realized that I was the one who gave her the candy. Over the years, I've mentioned it many times, and it's become kind of a standing joke whenever we see each other.

*Fred and Hendrik drive tiny Isetta automobiles through the aisles of the
Michigan and Fuller store in a promotion c. 1955*

"Have Fun"
Leadership isn't always serious

DISCRIMINATION

Russ Johnson was our first black manager.

We had a management seminar put on by a Mr. Phillips and Larry Taylor for the Super Market Institute in Chicago. The seminar included other company people, and it was held at the Edgewater Beach Hotel. I didn't know whether the Edgewater Beach would accept black people, and I was so concerned that I called ahead, and they said there won't be any problem, but I was still concerned and as an extra safety precaution, I assigned Bud Clark, who was one of our better and more seasoned store managers. I said "Bud, you be the head of this group, and if in any way Russ Johnson gets insulted, misused or doesn't get fully as good a service as the rest of you, I want you all to come home en masse. Just check out and tell them that you aren't going to be a party to it."

Well, there was no problem, but this is how concerned we were about potential problems along those lines.

While I'm on the subject of race relations, to go back to the Fuller store, #6, when we were going to hire a receptionist who also answered the telephone, Harvey Lemmen came to me and said I have three applicants that I've screened it down to. I feel any of the applicants would be okay, but I'd like your advice as to which one to hire."

And I said, "Gee, Harvey, don't worry about it. Just hire the one you think is best."

"Well, let me just review it with you. One is black."

"Well," I said, "What's the problem?"

He says, "Well, I've had comments that some people say if we get a black lady in the office, they want separate toilets and so forth."

I said, "If we're going to be prejudiced, let's just tell her we're prejudiced, and we aren't ready yet for a black receptionist."

He said, "But I have had some adverse comments, what do I do?"

I said, "Well, what would you like to do, Harvey?" He said, "I would like to hire her."

Now, if he'd have said, "I would prefer not to hire her, I'd like to skip it," I think I would have said okay. When he said he would like to hire her, I said okay.

I said, "I will talk to each person in the office so that if we hire

Fred and Hendrik make a presentation to an associate at a company Christmas dinner c. 1951

her we will treat her decently, or we'll tell her our people are too prejudiced."

That would have been illegal, but I wasn't thinking of the law. I was only thinking of the human side of it, and it probably would have been better to hire her even if there had been prejudice, because she needed the job, but I wasn't thinking of that either. So I went to the first person in the office and then another person and another person until I covered pretty well the whole office. I would tell the story that we had a black person apply, we'd prefer to hire her, how did they feel about it? Some people would say, "Oh, I don't care." Others would say, "It doesn't matter, whatever you think." Others would say, "I don't mind for myself, but the other ones might not like it."

I had several comments like that, and my stock answer was, "Then I'll put you down as 'you don't mind for yourself' because you see, I'm going to talk to all the others, and you don't need to speak for them, just speak for yourself."

Nobody had nerve enough to say, "We don't want her, and after I got halfway through the office, I think the word went out Fred Meijer is doing this and this and this, and I didn't have anybody else say that they didn't want her, and so we hired her, and it worked out just fine. With that we got a reputation for hiring a black person without being pushed.

During this time, the Urban League was urging and pleading to hire black people because black people couldn't get work, and here we come along and hire black people without anybody urging us to do it. This was a departure from the normal, and so Paul Phillips came over and wanted to know what we were doing. We got better acquainted, and the first thing I knew, I was on the board of directors of the Urban League. I was on their employment committee and in addition to that, he had me speaking on how to properly hire minority people.

Actually, our program was so simple and so direct. The interesting part of it was, if everybody made it simple and direct, there probably wouldn't be a problem. We make it complicated way beyond the problem, usually. Well, anyway, that started me off with a reputation for working with ethnic groups, which I am still doing in one capacity or another.

Many years later, when we had the Thrifty Acres stores, probably about 1963 or so--this was back in '52 when we opened the Fuller stores, so that's 11 years later--I was in Florida and went into a discount store there called the Jefferson Store. I had to go to the bathroom and the first door I came to was ladies, so I sailed in the next door and that was still ladies. There was Kotex on the wall and so forth, and I was embarrassed and I got out of there and I looked at the next door and that was men. I went in there and used the facility and then I came out to see what the heck I had done why I made the mistake, and so I looked and there was "ladies," "ladies," "mens," "mens," with a little blank spot above the ladies and the men and then I see where it was--then I realized what had happened. They had taken off the words "white women," "colored women," "white men," "colored men" and just had "women," "women" or "ladies," "ladies"--and that was one of my little experiences with the changing race problems in the South.

I also remember driving to the South somewhere along this time when the gas station in the rural area would have "women, men" for toilets on the side and a flag sticking out saying "colored." Behind the gas station would be "colored men, colored women." Complete separate toilets. That always struck me as being very wrong.

Fred wears a director's badge at a convention of the Super Market Institute (now the Food Marketing Institute), c. 1959. He is FMI's senior active director

MORE GOOD THAN HARM

I can remember some of the mistakes I made. I used to make out most of the ads in the very, very early days. Later on Lena helped me a lot with the ads, and my dad always helped with the headline, but I wrote the ads before Lena and I wrote them together, and I made a mistake on butter in the ad and I advertised it way below cost, and I went to my dad all red-faced and told him about the mistake. I wanted to run a correction in the ad in the paper saying we'd made a mistake, and that butter wasn't supposed to be advertised at that price, but my dad says don't run a correction. Let her go at that price. Let the people feel we got a real hot bargain, and maybe it will do us more good than harm, and actually it did come out that way.

STAMPS

It's hard to change religions I guess, although I've never tried it. But we were on cash and trying to have the lowest prices, then we went into something called premium coupons, P.C. That was kind of a pseudo trading stamp—you saved your tape and you got premiums. And then Lena and I went to a convention in 1956 or somewhere in there, and we heard them say stamps are worth more than their cost because people value them so highly— it motivates them to trade with you. And at that time Mr. Eberhard had gone into S&H stamps and he was mowing competition down. So I came back in '56 recommending that we go into stamps. We researched them all and we started our own called Goodwill. We were in them for about three years, and in 1960 I went to my dad and said, "I think maybe we ought to get back to our pricing," because stamps did cost 2 percent and we were constantly seeing how could we raise the margin to cover the stamp cost. And I didn't realize how anti-stamps my dad was. I said, "I think we ought to wait until after Christmas, till people get their coupons and their gifts to get out of stamps." He said, "I agree with you totally. I think we ought to go out of them right now." Golly, I could hardly hold him back. Well, within about eight weeks, we were out of stamps. We went to the bank and said we don't know what is going to happen to our business, will you hold our hand and loan us money in case we lose business? As it was, we cut prices and this was one of the best things we ever did. It was like getting back to basics. I led the company into stamps; I took total responsibility, I talked them into it, everybody agreed or we wouldn't have done it. But basically I led them out.

CHAPTER 5
~
THE 60s

A newspaper artist captured facets of Fred's personality in this 1969 cartoon drawn soon after he became local chairman of the JOBS program, a national effort to employ the jobless

At left, associates mark down prices to dramatize the company's decision in 1960 to abandon trading stamps in favor of more hotly competitive pricing

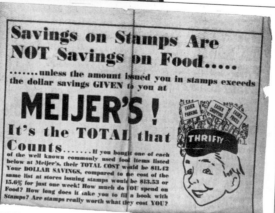

July 25, 1960

8.

Pat & Harvey:

With Reference to Leonard St. Produce Dept.

6:30 P.M. Sat. the rack was ½ bare, the floor was littered, the carrots & other items needed water. The dept. needed straighening out & policing. A lot could be done in 15 Min. of fussing but I don't think the boy knew how.

Please check on this & give me a report.

Fred Meijer

Reflecting the attention to detail so critical to successful retailing, Fred passed this note to colleagues after a routine store visit in 1960

GROCERS' SPOTLIGHT

The Newspaper of the MICHIGAN Food Market

VOL. 27 — NO. 14   JUNE 6 1960   707 FOX BLDG., DETROIT 1, MICHIGAN

Meijer-Plumb Merger Produces $37 Million Firm; 23 Stores

Disagreement over valuation of the two chains' respective real estate holdings led to the collapse of a planned merger between Meijer and Muskegon-based Plumb Supermarkets in 1960. Above, Fred signs the initial agreement with Plumb chairman Norris Plumb while (from left) Harvey Lemmen, Don Magoon, Johanna Magoon and Plumb executive Bill Dorr look on

THRIFTY ACRES

We were outside of the Fuller Store, coming back from someplace. Dad sat in the car, I remember it so clearly. We'd been to New York, and we'd been all over looking at big stores, and I said, "Well, what would you do, now, if you were me? What would you do now? What do you think? What should we do?"

I knew he was enthusiastic about going all the way but he said, "Well, I don't think I'd do it."

I was completely surprised, because I knew he didn't mean what he said. I said, "Well, what do you mean?"

"I'm too old."

"Oh," I said, "Well, what would you do if you were me at my age?"

He said, "I'd jump in with both feet."

He was saying, "If we go broke, and I die, I don't want you to blame me. I want it to be your decision."

"Now, if you decide you'd like to do it, which I'd like to see you do, I'd like to be part of it. I'll commit everything I got."

He would stake everything. If we went broke, it didn't matter. He was so sold it would work, he was willing to gamble, but he wasn't willing for me to blame him. I think it was quite a message.

NAMING THE BIG STORE

We operated as Meijer Super Markets once we dropped the Thrift Market name, and when we ran a contest in 1961 for names for our department store venture, the name Thrifty Acres, a derivative of our old Thrift Market days, was suggested by Fred Welling.

My dad would come home and say, "Well, you got any names we can call this thing?" and I'd come up with a few silly suggestions, and then one day he came home and said, "We've got it," and that was it.

FIVE-INCH CONCRETE FLOORS

The Muskegon store has a five-inch reinforced concrete floor, so if we ever failed there, we could turn it into an automobile dealership and would not crush the floor. We did the same thing in Holland and in Grand Rapids. The addition at

The first big "Thrifty Acres" store opened on 28th Street at Kalamazoo Avenue in Grand Rapids in June 1962. The original supermarket occupied the arch-roofed structure at lower left

Kalamazoo and 28th Street was completely separated from the supermarket in case we failed because we were anticipating the possibility of failure. Then without realizing it, as we built more stores, we built them all with five-inch floors, forgetting our reason. Then we said, "Well, my gosh, we are not building garages here, we are building retail stores. We do not need a five-inch reinforced floor. Four inches is enough," so we went back and saved an inch on the concrete.

FROM AN INTERVIEW IN *GROCERS' SPOTLIGHT*, FEBRUARY 5, 1962

Normally quiet and soft-spoken, Meijer will not stand for the use of the word "discount" in connection with Thrifty Acres. "In the first place," he points out, "the term itself is becoming less realistic all the time. When Fair Trade laws held sway, a written-in lower price on a manufacturers price tag meant something. The customer could see the difference. But this never did hold true on soft goods, and now manufacturers are abandoning the old price tag anyway."

"In the second place," Meijer continues, "we have been carrying non-food and soft goods for years. They have always been priced competitively with any discount store, but would you call us a discount store now?"

Now out of stamps for over a year, Meijer smiles at the memory.

"We have got nothing against stamps," he said, "I save them myself. But with everybody giving them away, it seemed that we might appeal to quite a few people who would rather save cash. We were a bit worried when we stopped, but our experience has borne us out. As it is now, we have a unique selling advantage in no-stamp prices, and it is a genuine one, too. On the average, our prices are lower."

"Not on every single item every day, of course--there are always specials and exceptions. If a shopper wants to take the time and trouble to seek them out, that is all right with us as long as she ends her tour at a Meijer store to stock up on all the non-specials at average lower prices."

TAKING OFF

We just wildly took over all these departments. And I can remember we sent a guy named Albert Meijer--no relation but same last name--to New York, and he bought on credit a quarter of a million dollars worth of stuff.

We didn't know if it was good, bad or indifferent, and luckily he was careful. He used pretty good judgment, and we squeaked through.

We pretty near went broke about three times since we had the Thrifty Acres stores. I mean, if you think we were in trouble with the supermarket or in the grocery store, we were in equal trouble with these big stores but the dollars were fantastic, comparatively.

Thrifty Acres' exhaustive list of goods and services in this 1962 grand opening ad includes, in alphabetical order, "lingerie, luggage, meats and men's furnishings." The name Meijer is nowhere to be found

CASH FLOW

In the early days of Thrifty Acres we didn't quite have our--
"not quite" is an understatement--we didn't have our cash
flow figured out, and so we ran out of money badly and
couldn't pay our bills again. We needed $2 million right now
to pay bills that we'd already incurred. We were running
behind in meeting our accounts payable. At that time, Mr. Ed
Barnes had been handling our account with the Michigan
National Bank, and understood our situation more thoroughly
than anyone else did at Michigan National. He went on a several weeks' trip golfing in Europe and about a day or two after
he left, we went into the bank and said, "We need $2 million,
and we need it right now."

Well, banks don't like to make up their mind that fast and
the one thing we know is, banks like a little advance notice.
They like to know what you're doing ahead of time so that
they can anticipate your problem, and not be slapped with it
quickly when you're already over the barrel. This is what we
were doing to the bank so they suggested we wait until Mr.
Barnes get back. We said we couldn't wait. So Mr. Joe Shaw
and Mr. Waldo Stoddard worked with us, and after a week or
two of work, we finally got the $2 million, but they had us tied
up in every way. We pledged everything we owned.

We personally endorsed the paper--I personally endorsed
the paper--and if we'd made one slip, theoretically, the bank
could have taken everything away from us. I signed my name
99 times. If we'd just stubbed our toes, we'd have lost everything. Everything. But we didn't stub our toe. We opened the
first Thrifty Acres in 1962. The first one in June and second
one in August, in Holland and Muskegon.

When I said to Mr. Stoddard I thought they were being
pretty tough and pretty tight on tying us down, he says,
"Fred, we don't want your business, all we want is our money
back and 6 percent interest."

I could understand, as I looked back on it, that banks had
seen people get into financial jams many times, and they knew
if they didn't tie them down tightly, and if a person wasn't
responsible, somebody might take that $2 million and head off
for Brazil or someplace, which has been done in some cases.
So they tied us down hand and feet.

Fred (rear left) saddles up with Hendrik and colleagues for a pre-opening pony ride in the new Thrifty Acres store, May 1962. Other riders include Harold Hans (front center), Bill Smith (front right) and Fred Welling (second from left). (The vendor's price for a pony ride had not yet been reduced to reflect the Meijer penny-pony commitment)

Grand opening of the first big store, 5 June 1962

I squirmed, but I vowed that I was going to try to have us run our business so that we would never get in that position again. And so that's when we went to making projections. We had, by then, good certified statements, but we didn't have good projections on cash flow to know when we were getting into trouble.

A few years later, we got into a bind again. We learned that not only do we need good statements and good projections, we need a calculated cushion for the present and some margin for error in case your sales didn't come through, the profits didn't come through, or something happened.

At that time, when we needed $2 million, I went to New York to talk to the credit people. There's about a half a dozen credit people in New York that recommend whether or not suppliers should sell to you. The biggest one, I believe, is Dun and Bradstreet, and the second biggest one is Credit Exchange, and there are several smaller ones.

I went to Dun and Bradstreet, explained to them that we had the bank loans to pay our bills and so forth, and a man named Ackerbloom says, "Well, here's our problem. We still can't recommend your credit, and here's why." And he showed me, in detail, why they couldn't recommend our credit: how we were slow in paying this account, and that account, and how our balance sheet was weak, and our current ratio of assets versus liabilities, and our cash positions were weak. Now, he said, if you'll do this and this and this, then we can recommend your account again. And so I went away from there vowing to do those things, and we did them. We straightened out our credit within a matter of a month or so.

Then I went to Credit Exchange and Mr. Meyering--I remember his name so well--he's probably retired now--was just the reverse of Mr. Ackerbloom. Mr. Ackerbloom helped me and was nice, and Mr. Meyering was kind of short and snippy and said, "Well, it's in the computer that way, and we can't get it out right away."

He did nothing to help me, and I went away from his office feeling very badly. What a difference in the way a person can be treated. I came all the way from Grand Rapids to New York

The world and 28th Street

From one side of the world, we tell of despotism and an experiment in human misery. From the other, Thrifty Acres on Grand Rapids' busy 28th Street, we report the benefits of super-store merchandising. Their differences are dramatic but each gives potent stimulation to our aim: to keep our listeners and viewers among the best-informed, best-served and best-entertained people in the world. To do this, we have the use of an awesome array of talent and facilities

— our own staff and equipment, the far-flung resources of Time-Life Broadcast and the full scope of NBC. How well we are succeeding may be measured by the ratings we get and the awards we win — more by the respect and confidence we have earned from the two million WOODlanders we serve.

WOOD AM · FM · TV *Grand Rapids, Mich.*
TIME-LIFE BROADCAST, INC.

WOOD · THE STATION WITH 2,000,000 CLOSE FRIENDS ██ NATIONAL SALES REPRESENTATIVES · THE KATZ AGENCY, INC.

This 1963 promotional ad for a local broadcaster contrasts Fred and Hendrik with another radical, Chairman Mao. (Only one of the three wears an open shirt, its pocket filled with pads and pens)

to talk about our credit. One man treated me like a gentleman and helped me. And the other one treated me, I thought, rude-ly, and didn't help me, and I just never forgot that.

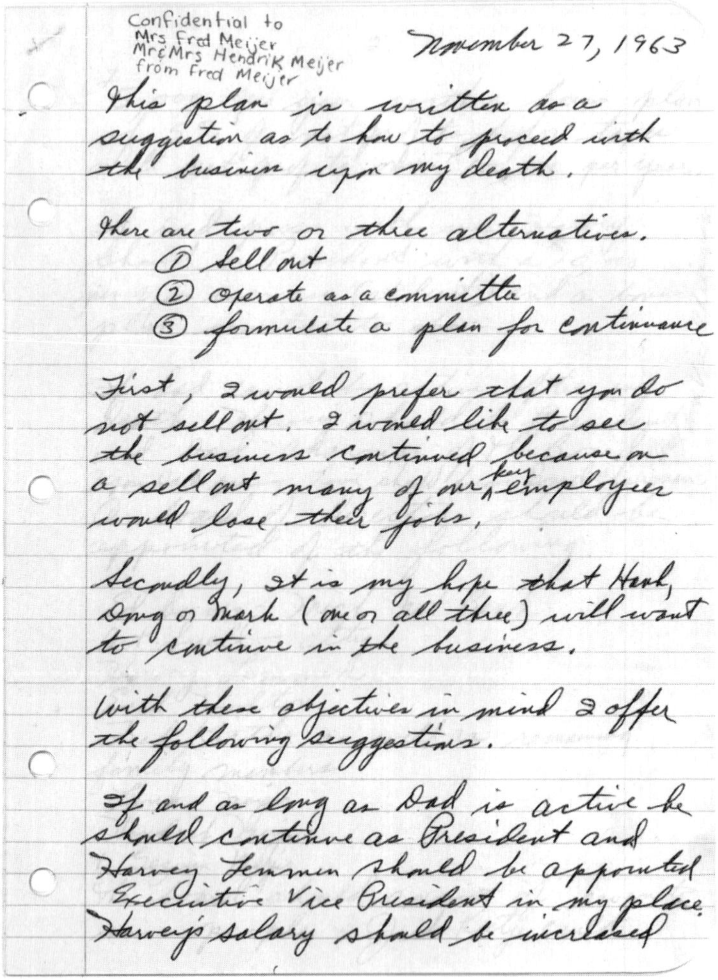

Confidential to
Mrs Fred Meijer
Mr&Mrs Hendrik Meijer   November 27, 1963
from Fred Meijer

This plan is written as a suggestion as to how to proceed with the business upon my death.

There are two or three alternatives.

① Sell out

② Operate as a committee

③ formulate a plan for continuance

First, I would prefer that you do not sell out. I would like to see the business continued because on a sell out many of our key employees would lose their jobs.

Secondly, It is my hope that Harl, Doug or Mark (one or all three) will want to continue in the business.

With these objectives in mind I offer the following suggestions.

If and as long as Dad is active he should continue as President and Harvey Lemmen should be appointed Executive Vice President in my place. Harvey's salary should be increased

HANDWRITTEN THOUGHTS, NOVEMBER 27, 1963

From: Fred Meijer
To: Mrs. Fred Meijer
       Mr. & Mrs. Hendrik Meijer

This plan is written as a suggestion as to how to proceed with the business upon my death.

There are two or three alternatives:
1. *Sell out*
2. *Operate as a committee*
3. *Formulate a plan for continuance*

First, I would prefer that you do not sell out. I would like to see the business continued because on a sellout many of our key employees would lose their jobs.

Secondly, it is my hope that Hank, Doug, or Mark (one or all three) will want to continue in the business.

With these objectives in mind, I offer the following suggestions.

If and as long as dad is active, he should continue as President and Harvey Lemmen should be appointed Executive Vice President in my place. Harvey's salary should be increased $5,000 per year with a bonus plan of 5 percent of net profits before taxes on all net profits over $100,000 per year.

If dad passes with me, Harvey should be President with a $10,000 per year increase (at least) and a bonus plan similar to above.

If dad cannot be active after my death, Harvey should be President and dad Chairman of the Board with Lena Vice Chairman. Upon dad's passing, Lena should become Board Chairman. A Board of Directors should be appointed of the following:

Ed Barnes - Michigan National Bank
Art Snell - Attorney
Harvey Lemmen
Earl Holton
Fred Kistler, as well as remaining family members
Lena Meijer
Hendrik Meijer
Gezina Meijer

The board should consist of seven to nine people. Jack Koetje could also possibly be added.

Harvey (if he is president) should appoint Earl Holton or Darrell Smucker as Merchandise Manager.

Jack Koetje or Earl Holton could also be Executive Vice President and the other Operations Director or Merchandise Manager. Jack Koetje is a good man; don't overlook his abilities.

As Hank, Doug, and Mark become active, I would like to see them be a member of the Board of Directors when it is felt they are old enough to contribute (if they are interested).

If the business cannot be operated at a profit then, of course, the Board of Directors should arrange the best possible sellout plan that will provide for Lena and our family and also protect mother and dad's notes due them and also pay off the notes due the Magoon family.

The timing of such a sellout should be after a sincere effort is made to continue, but before it is too late to save most of our investment.

If after Hank, Doug, and Mark have all passed age 21 and if they do not show interest in staying with the business then, if practical, the company should sell stock and become a public company.

More will be added to this set of notes as conditions change or new thoughts occur.

Frederik Meijer

Since November 27, 1963, my father has passed away and my mother is now President.

As long as she cares to be active, we should continue her on the payroll. Upon my death she should be named Chairman of the Board and Harvey Lemmen should become president.

Harvey's salary should be increased $10,000 per year plus a bonus of 2-1/2% of the net profit in pre tax earnings over $400,000 with a ceiling on his pay of $45,000 at which point his pay would drop to 1% of the net profit with a ceiling maximum of $60,000. Earl Holton and other key people should be increased in salary also so we don't lose key people.

Share objectives & problems

In a partnership that continued until Hendrik's death in May 1964, father and son shared an office and an outlook on life

WORKING TOGETHER

When we wanted to accomplish something, we'd talk over how we were going to do it. Then he would send me out to do it, and I'd quite often be very afraid of the job. But he'd say, "You can do it. Here's how to do it," and by golly, I was able to do things that I didn't realize I was able to do and we probably got a better job done having me do it than he doing it--at least that was his strategy. I learned and he delegated.

He very much believed in the dignity of people. When he talked about his foundry experiences in the west, when so many nationalities washed up in one pail, he often said everybody could get along in the world if we of different races could get along and respect each other in the foundry.

WHAT SIZE IS THE RIGHT SIZE?

We built the South Division store by going to the Old Kent Bank for a $25,000 mortgage and going to the Smith Lumber Company and arranging for a small contractor to build on a cost-plus basis.

We had radiant heat in the floor, which was quite new and we made the size of the store 10,000 square feet because we had come to the conclusion that 12,000 square feet was too large. It's interesting over the years that we overbuilt the Ionia store, supposedly, at 12,000 feet, then went back to 10,000 feet on South Division. In subsequent years we would raise that store on Division to 15 and then to 20,000 feet and the Ionia store to 17,000, but we went up and down. Then the Eastern Store was 14,500 feet, which then we thought was a good supermarket.

Then our Fuller store was more like 20,000 feet on the main floor. Of course we had offices upstairs and a warehouse in the basement. Then we went to 19,000 square feet at Rogers Park. Then we went to #10, which was about 20,000 square feet, on Leonard. We experimented with a downtown store, and then Standale we made 17,500 square feet. And then we went from there to #11 which we made 16,000 square feet. We made it smaller. That's the original arch-roofed store.

And then #12 at Plainfield was 22,000 square feet, because that was one wing of the old Helms building. We remodeled an old garage on Sanford in Muskegon and made that about 14,000 square feet, then we built #15 in Muskegon and we went all the way up to 21,000 square feet. Then #16 in Battle Creek and #17 in Holland and #18 in Grand Haven--we made them all about the same at 14,500 square feet. We thought that 20,000 feet was too big.

So over the years we went up and down and up and down. Later on we opened the first Thrifty Acres--enlarged #11 to make it 100,000 feet. The Muskegon Thrifty Acres was 100,000 and Holland we enlarged to 67,000. By the time we got those going and opened the two stores in Kalamazoo, we thought that 70,000 was more right than 100,000 so we made those two stores each 70,000.

By the time we got to Lansing with store #23, we thought 100,000 was better again, and we started construction on #23 and #24 at 100,000 and then, while we were building them, decided that we ought to make them 150,000. At the same time we added on to Alpine and made that first 100,000 and then 150,000 and then we jumped all the way from there to 220,000. Then we cut back in the Flint and Jackson stores to 160,000 and 180,000, and then we jumped up in the Detroit stores to 240,000, and now we've cut back a little bit again.

So we've been up and down like a yo-yo.

First I don't like to make speeches,
it makes me think

Second I do like to make speeches
just because they do make me think

DON'T WORRY, HAVE FUN

Another thing I've learned but don't always practice is not to fret over those things over which I have no control. And conversely, work on those things over which I can effect some changes. In that way you don't fret about the impossible or the undoable, and you work on the possible and the doable. You save a lot of time. Hopefully, you get fewer ulcers, and you have a lot more fun out of life. I remember telling an Armour executive once, when he asked me what I thought it took to have a practical or a successful business and I said-- just on the spur of the moment without thinking through deeply--three things that I can quickly think of.

First, you have to have a company that's needed today, because if you didn't have someplace a customer wanted to shop or if you're producing tires--if nobody wanted your tires--you'd be out of business anyway.

Second, you need a product line or a service that hopefully will be needed 5-10-15 years from now, because if you don't have, you're going to have to do some fast changing or the people who earn their livelihood at it are going to lose their jobs, and the people that loaned you money might not get their money back.

Third, you should have a company in which people can have fun. Now fun can be labeled in several different ways, but the fun I'm talking about is job satisfaction--human satisfaction--the feeling that what you're doing has some meaning, and if we can have this feeling or be given this feeling or acquire this feeling, then the job will become what I call fun.

I really feel sorry for someone who finds no "fun" in their work, because life must be pretty dull. And in fact, unless you're just locked in in a way you can't get out, if a job doesn't give you any satisfaction, certainly you ought to change to one that will give you satisfaction.

Don't Hate - understand

"Getting there is all the fun," from the dunk tank to a sack race, c. 1964. Climbing into the burlap at a company picnic are (from left) Fred, Paul Casper, Harold Hans, Carl Graczyk, Mal Harrington and Jim Anderson

UNIONS

Shortly after we opened the Eastern Store, there was a very intense unionizing drive. I remember them walking into my office, the people from the butcher's union and the retail clerk's union. Never said hello or anything. Just walked right over to my feet, practically, grabbed my phone, used the long distance phone--real strong arm tactics, talking to somebody, supposedly. Said, "Close them up. Strike them. Do this, do that. Close the sons of bitches up," and so forth. Then they slammed down the phone, and they said, "Hello."

I said to them, "That's quite a show you put on there."

And it was real interesting, because then my dad and Van came in the office and they (the union men) were all sweetness and light. Just turned on the charm. But a few minutes before that, they'd used our phone without asking for a long distance call, used all kinds of strong conversation and profanity.

Anyway, they tried to get us to sign up the employees, which was a favorite way in those days. They said, "If you sign your employees you can make the bastards climb that wall or whatever you want the sons of bitches to do, they got to do."

My dad says, "Now wait a minute, since when are we calling our employees those kinds of names? We don't talk about our people that way. We don't feel about our people that way, and we don't like you talking about them that way."

They were going from store to store telling different stories, most of them untrue, that we had this signed up, and we had that signed up and so forth until finally some employees said, "We'd like to start our own union, and we don't like this kind of harassment, and you say you would sign with them if they represented us." We said, "Well, we'd have to." They were threatening to fine anybody who didn't join and so forth. Well, anyway, the upshot of it was Federal Mogul had an independent union in Greenville and the same attorney that worked on that, they went to him, and they organized their own union. That was the start of the Consolidated Independent Union.

FROM A LETTER TO HENDRIK
JUNE 27, 1960

Tonight there is our second union meeting on new rates. Last week they gave us their high proposal. Tonight we give them our low

Fred and colleagues sign a new contract in 1966 with Local 951 of the Consolidated Independent Union. Front row center are Gezina Meijer and union president Milo Fifield. Among those representing the company are Chuck Westra, Earl Holton, Harold Hans, Jack Koetje and Bill Smith

counter proposal and then we will get down to business.

Louise, Hank, Doug, Scott and Steve are playing ball in the back yard. Lena is rocking Mark on the back porch on the rocking porch swing. When she stopped a moment he said let's go rock some more, let's go rock to Holland.

BANKERS

We've dealt with, I would guess, 30 banks over the years, and probably deal with 25 of those 30 right now and only one demanded its money back when they thought we had financial problems. All the rest of the banks, when we explained our problems, worked to help us get out of the problem.

I can't help but remember how that one wanted its money back. We did talk them into taking it back over a period of four or five months, but I'll never forget that when the chips were down, they closed in.

And this, of course, is sometimes what gives bankers a bad reputation, but we should always keep in mind that in dealing with 30 banks and probably twice that many bankers over the years, only one has treated us roughly and that's pretty good.

*Meijer board members c. 1969: (from left) Harvey Lemmen, attorney
Art Snell, Gezina, Fred, Lena, banker Ed Barnes and Earl Holton*

ED BARNES, DIRECTOR

When Mr. Barnes had attended our board meetings for the better part of a year, he said to me after one meeting, "Fred, I don't think it's necessary that I come to these board meetings anymore."

Knowing that he was a busy man, I said, "Well, I understand, Mr. Barnes, you're busy, and if you don't have time, we sure appreciated the months of board meetings that you have attended."

"Well, it's not that I don't have time, it's just that it's no longer required."

Then I learned that as a part of the condition of this loan, Mr. Barnes had to attend our board meetings to look after things, and if I had refused, they probably would have said, "Well, Fred, if you want this loan, this is what you have to do."

But I didn't refuse. I welcomed them. I think if I'd have refused completely, they probably would have turned us down on the money. I didn't realize that until almost a year later.

Fred encouraged his mother's active participation in company affairs after Gezina succeeded her husband as president in 1964

CREDIT

Twice in the last 15 years, we have gone to the bank and told them that we would be agreeable to them raising our interest rates even though they were locked in at a certain rate. We said to them, "Interest rates have gone up substantially, and we have a right to pay off. Had they gone off substantially, we'd have paid you off and demanded or requested a lower interest rate. Because they've gone up substantially, we would be agreeable to raising your rate." I think they were quite surprised that any of their customers would raise their own cost of money.

Don't Demand or expect the impossible

SANDY THE PONY

A fellow named Bob Newman who had supermarkets in Omaha, Nebraska, said, "Fred, I've got an idea for you for your store (this was before we went into the big store). We've done this and we've had a good reception of it." That was the pony ride—except they were charging a dime, and the more we thought about it in those days, a dime was a lot of money, a dime then was more than a quarter is now.

If you've got three kids and they each want a quarter ride, you've got to put in 75 cents and you're almost going to cuss the store for having the horse there. If you can put a penny in you can be a hero to the kids for a penny, or for three cents for three kids.

One of the funniest things I ever saw was just the other day when we went to Benton Harbor. We were in the Benton Harbor store and [Frederik Meijer Garden director] Mark Jeter's three-year-old twin daughters wanted to ride the pony. So what do they do, they both want to get on the pony—one sits on the pony and rides and the other one backs up to the pony and lets it kick her in the bottom with its tail. I would like to have had a video of that. Basically it just makes shopping more fun.

If we can treat people right, shopping becomes a pleasure, and if we can give them good service, shopping becomes a pleasure, and then we can offer them amenities like the pony...When we had a fire once little kids cried when Sandy the pony got burned. It was quite emotional.

PURPLE COW

I remember seeing a purple cow in a restaurant in Dayton when we went down to a National Cash Register Seminar. I also always liked that poem, "I never saw a purple cow, and never hope to see one...."

SANITATION

No matter how low our prices are, people wouldn't shop here if the store wasn't clean. If I wouldn't buy my food here, I wouldn't expect anyone else to come here either.

Long before the opportunity arose for a presidential museum in Grand Rapids came this photo, c. 1969, of (from left) Lenore Romney, Michigan Governor George Romney, Lena, Fred and U.S. Representative Gerald R. Ford

THE FORD MUSEUM

I really didn't know President Ford that well until we started the museum. Then he was a hometown person, and a group of us were asked to start it and I ended up being vice chairman, and chairman of the site selection committee. There were about four of us that were the real wheel horses who met every week. As a matter of fact, I couldn't get the President's interest, because he wouldn't do a thing while he was running for reelection, because it was too premature. Jimmy Carter beat him, and then he wouldn't do a thing between the November elections and the January swearing in. January came along and he was just out of office and it was quite a let down I think, or a change of life, and he still didn't seem to be ready. So they sent me to Florida with Dick Ford, Jerry's half-brother, and we had to get his attention, say, "Hey, do you want a museum?" So we got his attention. Then we have to get cracking. I hired a plane. Meijer paid for it, chartered it to go to Hoover's and Truman's and Eisenhower's libraries.

KEEP INFORMED

Now you have to work through people who work through people and you have to work with people who work with people. And it is that sort of thing that frustrated my dad when he was about 80 years old. He said, "Nobody listens to me any more." This was frustrating to him. Later in my dad's life, I would come back from vacation and all heck would break loose. It had broken loose while I was gone: my dad was being unreasonable, he was finding fault, and he wasn't that kind of guy.

So finally I figured out what it was. I had seven people responsible to me, Earl Holton, Harvey Lemmen, Van Valkenburg the meat man, and the produce man, the advertising manager and personnel. They would work with me, and I kept my dad informed. I realized his need to be in on things but also, by keeping him informed, I got his advice and consent, and we'd accidentally worked into what I'd call a very beautiful working relationship. Well, while I was gone, nobody told him what was going on. So finally I said to these people, Stop in and tell my dad a little something that is going on so that he knows he is in the loop. He probably won't want to listen to much, because he'll say, "Well, you run it," but at least he can get a feel for what is going on. After they did that I had no more problems, just no more problems. Basically he was lonesome and if he couldn't be part of things, he'd go out and find trouble.

I think the moral is that if you don't involve people in your problems, they will go to somebody else to help them. If you can involve people in your problems, they'll help you. It is not a weakness to say, "I don't know, will you help me?" It is not a weakness to say, "I need you."

We have almost 60,000 people working with us. We need them, so let's treat them like we need them. Everybody responds to the feeling that we are needed. We want to be considered intelligent human beings. If we make a mistake, we don't need to be bawled out, we need to be helped to succeed. I don't know how many thousands of management people we have, but if we can have them feel that their job isn't to boss people around, their job isn't to manage, their job is to help people succeed. If they can help them succeed, their job will be better and everybody will be more productive.

CHAPTER 6

~

THE 70s

OVEREXPANSION

We proceeded to open the enlarged area of the Alpine Store and the two new 150,000 square feet stores in Lansing. At the same time, we added some warehousing in Grand Rapids, and we did not borrow enough money to cover all these additions. We used what little working capital we had, and we could not pay our bills.

We went what they call, "slow" in the trade. If a bill was due in 10 days, we might take 20 to pay it. If a bill was due in 30 days, we might take 45 or 60 to pay it. Well, when you go slow in paying your bills, that word goes out awfully fast: "Meijer's got trouble." You had other companies like Arlan's and Miracle Mart in serious financial troubles, and later on Grant's and Yankee's and Zody's and Shopper's Fair, many of whom went through bankruptcy. A company like us, not that big in relation to the total, may be very big to a supplier. They are a very small company and cannot afford to take a $1,000 loss.

When they say a company is slow in the trade, it is risky. A company that has been burned a couple of times might not ship. Some, then, in addition to that, will ship late. For example, if you need summer merchandise by the first of April, they will take care of all their customers that are going to pay promptly, and they might ship you the first of May or the first of June or even as late as the first of July. Or they will cancel your order and not even tell you they have cancelled. They just do not ship. Sometimes they do not want to tell you because they might hurt your feelings for future business, or they might say we will learn more on a future credit report; we will ship those people that are going to pay for sure and just hold up this order.

It is not so critical in the hard goods area because somehow the hard goods firms often are bigger firms and have their own credit departments and will take some chances. And it is not so critical in food because you do not go that long "slow" in the trade in food or you lose your cash discount.

But in the meantime, back in Grand Rapids, Michigan, we are waiting and depending on this merchandise to come, and it just does not arrive.

'Little' Chain Heads for the Big Time With 7 Detroit Superstores by '78

BY ELLEN HUME
Free Press Business Writer

ND RAPIDS — Fred
, president of a $350 mil-
grocery-discount chain,
s to pick up a soggy
ook cover while walk-
ess his parking lot with
r.

can't stand litter," he
carrying the dripping
o the nearest trash can.
gesture illustrated two
about Fred Meijer's ap-
to his family business:
y's attention to details
doesn't mind being so-

qualities will come in
during the next four
when Meijer Inc.
its assault in Detroit,
up seven huge Meijer
Acres stores around
skirts of the city by

E RETAILERS will
y say Fred Meijer is
After all, Detroit is no-
y overstored already.
six cutthroat grocery
And why should Meijer
as a mass merchandi-
K mart's back yard—

Thrifty Acres: Neither a K-mart nor a hypermarche. The secret's in being
both smaller and bigger than the competition

*Admitted "Flaming liberal"
Fred Meijer has some unu-
sual ideas about running a
business — like trying to
remember the names of all
his 7,000 employes and an
obsession with promoting*

*Fred's ambitions, as reflected in this 1974 headline, proved somewhat opti-
mistic. After the company opened three mammoth stores in the highly competitive Detroit area it still lacked the resources to expand quickly enough to
gain market share and reduce heavy advertising expenses*

FROM AN INTERVIEW IN THE *DETROIT FREE PRESS,* MARCH 31,1974

We do not claim to have prices that are lower than everybody else's. We just want to be equal to the best values. We
base our business on volume, but we do not have the buying
power of K-Mart. So, like the old Dutch saying, he who is not
strong has to use his head.

We are not out to conquer the world.

K-Mart is a dangerous example to try to copy. They put up
100 stores a year - that is two stores a week. We do not want to
kid ourselves.

I come from a family of flaming liberals.

When you are in business, you are where it is at. You provide jobs, goods, services. You can provide jobs that give more
opportunity to blacks, women and others. Then aren't you a
positive force in this society?

CANTON STORE

In 1974 we opened the Thrifty Acres on Ford Road in Detroit. With the Jackson store, we cut back to about 160,000 square feet because we thought the 220,000 at Okemos and Jenison was too big and--the 180,000 or 185,000 in Flint was too big so we cut back to 160,000, and now we're working out an enlargement because we thought that was too small, then we jumped all the way to 245,000 or 250,000 square feet at Ford Road. Now that's too big.

It seems like we're never happy with the store size after we get them opened. Ford Road has lost us a lot of money--is still losing money (In 1995, that was not the case). It was the fastest growing area in the Detroit area because it could get gas, and it was good building soil and then all at once, the credit crunch came in '73, plus the fact that they got a new supervisor who wouldn't allow any housing to be built west of our store and declared that was to stay forever farm land. With the slowing up of the building possibilities, due to zoning, and then with K-Mart and another shopping center with a big Kroger that set up a special zone just to be sure they were never undersold by our Ford Road prices--with all this competition, we didn't get the volume we should have. Our gross margin was too low. Our advertising costs were too high. We've lost tremendous sums of money since that store opened, but we've still got hopes for it.

PRICING

We just try to be the low man in the market. If you try to be lower than everybody, that's a sure way to go broke. But if you can be the lowest in relation to most people, that's the sure way to gain customer confidence, because they won't find us higher than this store, higher than that store, except on specials, we hope.

Billed as the "country's first hypermarket," Meijer store #32 opened in Canton Township, Michigan in 1974. It featured a party store, major appliances, and massive wire merchandising bins similar to those in the huge French stores known as "hypermarkets"

The soaring cost and occasional scarcity of gasoline, as reflected in this issue of the company's Cracker Barrel from 1978, helped throw Michigan's economy into a recession and made Fred and his colleagues more sensitive to issues of energy conservation and the environment

DON'T FEAR FAILURE

If you aren't willing to try and fail you won't try that next thing that is going to preserve the company. We've got to be careful, but we can't be afraid of failure or we'll never have success.

Fellow retail entrepreneur Fred Meyer, founder of the Fred Meyer chain of combination food and general merchandise stores in Portland, Oregon, tours the new Meijer automated warehouse in Lansing with Fred, c. 1976

NEGOTIATIONS

When we've negotiated leases, and been stuck on a single point, quite often I'd say, okay, let's set this down on a piece of paper. Let's go to the next one. If you've got 20 issues you're working on in a lease, whatever the little points and big points are, by the time you get pretty near all of them resolved, then some of the other ones don't seem quite as important, and you end up being able to negotiate them out. I think I've used that approach when I've had parties in a dispute. I would say, "Give me all your problems. Now, if we settle all of this, you going to be happy?" "Yeah." " Okay." Then we'd proceed to try to settle it. And then nobody raised their voice.

NO EXPERTISE

I do not think money equates to brains and I do not want to get into the position that people think just because we built these stores, now we ask Fred's opinion and it is worth more than if he did not build the stores. It does not make me an expert in anything. I was asked to talk to the Economics Club. I did not even take bookkeeping in high school, so I turned them down. Then later I agreed. Maybe I should talk because of the economic impact we might have on the community.

BEING PRUDENT

I do not like tags, but I discussed my philosophies back in the Vietnam days with an attorney in Washington who called me a conservative. I asked why, and he said I was trying to be realistic enough to have policies that will conserve the nation's or my own business more than those who think we have to strip out everything that is communistic or promote every-thing that is liberal. I would like to think I am trying to be prudent. I would not want to be labeled as a conservative or a liberal or anything else.

I do not like those labels.

YOU ARE IMPORTANT

I have had people tell me that if I were their employee, they would fire me. A business is only as good as the people in it, the ideals they contribute and the enthusiasm they pursue these ideals with. We believe in clean stores. We believe in hon-est dealing--we will never ask an employee to lie for us. If the stuff does not come in and we are out of stock, do not play games with the customer.

I think every employee is entitled to dignity, and this is what I like to talk about best. If you work here, are you expendable? No, you are important. If we treat you that way, you will treat the job that way. We believe in doing that with customers, with suppliers, with bankers, in all of our people relations.

I believe in promoting from within. Most of our key people here have grown up with the company. So many people over-look the acres of diamonds. They go outside to hire a new sales manager or new president. I have seen it done time and time again.

HARD WORK
It has been an interesting life and I would not have missed it for anything else in the world. But believe you me, it was a lot of hard work.

TICKLES
It tickles your ego to think that you are respected.

Did you ever notice, by the time a company leaves a community, closes its doors, they are hardly missed. Most customers fired them long ago.

RECYCLING

All the tonnage that we gather we used to burn, to throw the smoke up into the air. Now we're recycling it through the baling and compacting operation.

We gather up 135 tons of paper each week. It's even amazing to us. We have balers in the store for everything that the paper people will accept for reclaiming. All the other junk and the paper with asphalt in it or with wires in it that we can't recycle, that goes into a compactor and is hauled to the landfill. But it's amazing. We do recycle 135 tons of paper a week. It goes in these 900 pound bales.

We got an ecology award a couple weeks ago from Judge Swainson, our ex-governor. I didn't know it myself before that, but since we started with one recycling place in Lansing and then expanded it to all the stores, in the last year and a half five and a half million tons of glass have gone back to be recycled and remelted and made into new bottles.

When we opened the first store in Greenville back in 1934, they used to laugh at us because we would sweep the sidewalk in front every day. We would sweep the gutter where the refuse would collect. Dad believed that if you didn't sweep the gutter it would blow right back on the sidewalk. He had been a barber and believed in cleanliness, so I guess I was indoctrinated from that standpoint.

We received an award for clean parking lots some time back. It never occurred to me that it was "environmental." I don't consider myself an environmentalist.

Our first store was built with used wooden lath. My job at 14 years old was to pull the nails out and chip the plaster off the wooden lath so we could reuse it. That was recycling.

Why did we do it? Because we were interested in recycling? No--we never even thought of that. It was because we were hard up. It was because labor was cheap and materials were expensive. Whenever labor becomes expensive and materials cheap, the incentive to recycle isn't there.

That's why if we're going to run out of gasoline or oil I'd like to see us have a dollar more on a gallon of gasoline right now. If we'd had a dollar more on a gallon of gasoline in '74, then we wouldn't be paying OPEC what we're paying today.

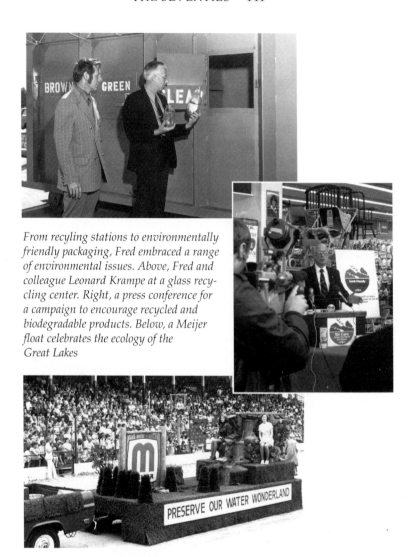

From recyling stations to environmentally friendly packaging, Fred embraced a range of environmental issues. Above, Fred and colleague Leonard Krampe at a glass recycling center. Right, a press conference for a campaign to encourage recycled and biodegradable products. Below, a Meijer float celebrates the ecology of the Great Lakes

General Motors would have been producing smaller cars because consumers would have demanded it.

All of us in business should keep an eye on the future, but the future is nothing if we don't stay in business today. Our number one job is to stay in business and balance all these things. But our number one aim should be to be a good corporate citizen. I think these two goals are compatible.

SHORT OF MONEY

In order to stay in business, we have to get higher production. Certainly, we have to have better people, or we can't survive. Hopefully, our better pay and better fringe benefits, etc., will give us the better people and the better production so we can survive. We've been short of money ever since we started in the grocery business. We started short of money. So that's no surprise to me. I guess the problem is how short and what totals are we talking about and how does it affect your business.

We have to build our stores so that no matter what happens, we can stay in business, because if you don't have lots of competition when you go in, you'll probably have it a few years later. When you sign a 25-year mortgage, you have to look at the long range, not the short range.

AVOIDING LAYOFFS

In 1975 we were still living in hopes that we could save our store on the north side of Kalamazoo when we came to the final decision that we could not save Store #21. We had already opened up Store #16, the new Thrifty Acres in Battle Creek, and had hired new people to staff that store and would not have anyplace to take these people to. We did not want to lay off a whole crew, and so this is the only time we have ever built a brand new store just to keep from laying off a crew. Of course, we hoped we could make the new store on Gull Road, which is now #21, also profitable over the years, but if we had had our druthers, we would have built it someplace else where we hopefully could have made it profitable sooner.

The Gull Road store opened in the fall of 1976 and prior to this year, 1977, that was our last store. This year, in 1977, we opened a store in Traverse City, in a defunct Grant location which we purchased.

Keep your word

Fred is always ready to immerse himself in the challenges of building a corporate culture. His signature Purple Cow ice cream card (below) is popular with guests who, as he likes to say, are "kids under 100." The Gelett Burgess verse on the reverse side: "I never saw a purple cow,/ I never hope to see one;/ But I can tell you anyhow/ I'd rather see than be one."

FROM AN INTERVIEW IN THE *GRAND RAPIDS PRESS,*
DECEMBER 26, 1977

Nobody here at Meijer gets promoted because he or she is
black or an Indian or a woman. But if that person is at a level
with what is required for the job, then he or she gets it. Even
if he or she is slightly below that level, we might assume that
maybe some hidden prejudice of ours in the testing or evalua-
tion may exist, and we will try the promotion or appointment.
Sometimes this leads to another problem, which we have to be
willing to face and work with. In our zeal to give a person a
chance, we may have overestimated that person's ability. If he
or she cannot fulfill the obligations of the job, that person will
be removed. We have to be practical. If we have a lot of people
in jobs they cannot handle, we will not stay in business
very long.

Therefore, we probably face more civil rights actions than
most other companies. (It's hard for some people to face up to
the fact that they could not do the job or that they moved
ahead too fast. It is much easier on the ego to believe themselves the victims of prejudice, since that is so widespread.)

But we have always been able to show a good record and
have come out well. If we did not have this open hiring and
promotion policy, we might not have the accusations. But
what we are doing is right and we will continue doing it.

YOU EARN LOYALTY

You earn loyalty. You don't buy it. You try to tell somebody
something and if you do it, they'll believe you and if you
don't, they won't believe you. You can waste a lot of money on
advertising by trying to make people believe things that they
know aren't true in your stores. If you're going to have loyalty
and you're going to have a good image, you certainly have to
earn it. If you don't think so, you're just kidding yourself. We
like to make money, but it's actually a by-product of trying to
do the job right. If you do the job right, so that your company
is a credit to the community, tries to be fair with the customers, never does anything that is dishonest--we tell every
cashier we will never ask you to do one dishonest act. We

Long-time associate Art Farley (left) is recognized by Lena, Gezina and Fred at a 1976 awards banquet

want everybody to get correct change. We want everybody to get correct weight. We want everybody to get proper quality and whenever you know that isn't true, we want you to try to do something about it.

PRODUCTIVITY

We work on productivity, productivity, productivity. We have to, and this is the whole thing. On the other hand, how do you get productivity with poorly motivated people? I'm convinced you don't motivate people as much with wages as you do with humane treatment, except it's pretty hard to eat that--so you need both.

DO YOU WANT TO BE PRESIDENT?

Jack Hamady once said to my dad, "Hey, you ought to make Fred president."

My dad turned to me, "You want to be President?"

I said, "I do not know, I never thought of it."

We worked so well together that we did not care about titles. I have also realized that the people around me need those titles and I want them to have them. Nobody ever said they needed them, but that is why I made Harvey Lemmen president, and I intend to make Earl Holton president after Harvey, which is kind of dangerous to line it up that far ahead. Some of these fellows have to know where they are going. After all, I have three sons. Some of them might come in the business. One is coming in, and I do not want to have these fellows be threatened with that.

TITLES

I've been in the unique position. I've been the boss's son, and my dad wasn't going to fire me. I suppose he could have but he never seemed to want to. I don't think I gave him any reason, because I've always been sincere. Until he died he was president and I was executive vice president, just to give ourselves a title.

However, when you have non-family people in the organization, then I felt we needed to recognize people for their jobs, and that is why I wanted Harvey Lemmen to be executive vice president. So when my dad died we made my mother president and I said to Mother, "Do you want to be chairman?" That was so I could be president, so I could make Harvey Lemmen executive vice president. So we made her chairman. Then I wanted to make Earl Holton executive vice president, so I said to my mother, "Would you be willing to be chairman emerita, so I can be chairman so Harvey can be president so Earl can be executive vice president?" She said, "Fine with me." Then later on I was proposing that Harvey be chairman and Earl be president and they came to me, Harvey and Earl, and said "We think you ought to keep the chairmanship in the family, it is a family company." Earl said, "I will be happy if I can be president." And so we made Harvey deputy chairman

*With the move of Gezina to chairman emerita, Fred (pictured here c. 1975)
became chairman of Meijer, with Harvey Lemmen (left) as vice-chairman
and Earl Holton president*

— he picked the title — and Earl president, which he is today
along with chief operating officer, and so we've used titles that
way. More important than titles is how you treat people. But if
you can treat people right and then recognize them both ver-
bally in what they do, and by title in what they represent—
that is how I've used titles.

FROM AN INTERVIEW IN THE *TRAVERSE CITY
RECORD-EAGLE,* MAY 25, 1977
*Meijer said he doesn't believe in formal titles, and bases his
prejudice on his European upbringing. Both his parents were from
the Netherlands, and disliked any kind of class or racial prejudice,
he said.*
"I don't believe in 'Mr. this or Mr. that,' it's just another barrier."

THE CUSTOMER'S IN CHARGE

You get a hold of the store manager and you say, "Now, these three items I couldn't find. Will you find them for me?"

See, there's always a manager in charge, and then you make him run instead of you. And once you get the technique of that, he'll have everybody working for you, if you get the right guy.

SATISFACTION

I believe there's no one job in which you can get complete satisfaction and there's no one job in relation to all other jobs that you can get enjoyment from. I think you can get enjoyment from many, many jobs, and hopefully you'll have one of those many jobs that will give you enjoyment.

WHERE ARE THE THUMBTACKS?

Would you believe it? I was at our Ypsilanti store a week ago Sunday, and I tried to find, what the dickens was it? Oh, yeah, thumbtacks. They chased me all over our store, and finally I found out they were in the hardware department. We didn't have them in health and beauty care or with the paper and school supplies. For the life of me I can't figure out why we don't have them there, but it took me half an hour to find out, and everybody knew who I was, too. I shouldn't get any better service than you do, but sometimes I might. This time I had the same problem.

SOME THOUGHTS

• From all these experiences, I developed some philosophies that I call my own. Nobody's philosophies are really their own. But one is that there's really no bad weather. There's weather that is bad for what you want to do, but weather in itself isn't bad.

• If it's raining, and you want to go on a picnic, well, then, that's bad for the picnic. But if we need the rain on the crops, it's not bad weather. The same is true of animals. If a wolf would hurt you if you came into his country, that doesn't mean the wolf is a bad animal, it means that he's afraid, and you're in his home territory. Maybe you carry a gun, why shouldn't he be afraid?

• We used to call Indians savages, yet we pushed them out of

The Meijer mystique

Fred promotes human side of 'hypermarket' concept

By DAVID HAYES
Record-Eagle staff writer

TRAVERSE CITY — Fred Meijer says people sometimes laugh at him when he talks about his bathrooms, but the man who heads the Midwest's largest family-owned grocery chain is having the last laugh.

Whether it's Fred Meijer's fanaticism for minute detail, or the Meijer chain's revolutionary marketing techniques, the one-stop "hypermarket" concept which came to Traverse City Tuesday has been a winning formula across the state.

The Meijer chain has carved a sizable chunk out of the grocery and clothing industry in 13 Michigan cities, and has completed a metamorphosis from corner grocery store to $300 million a year industry in less than two decades.

And hoping to unite a disorganized on-again, off-again segment of Traverse City's shoppers, Meijer's spent a reported $4 million to buy and reconstruct the former Grants Department Store here.

Meijer hopes to capture that scattered portion of the area's shopping market with promises of lower market basket prices and some bargains he says which can't be duplicated this side of Grand Rapids.

But the 58-year-old "chief executive officer" of the Grand Rapids-based chain lets the Meijer name speak for itself. He doesn't actively promote the company's topsy-turvy marketing techniques, or the Meijer's reputation for low prices.

The $300 million industry is left in his office when Meijer shows visitors through the chain's latest addition — a building in Traverse City Meijer's spent more than $2 million rebuilding. The first exhibit on the tour is a $1,000 motorized grocery cart for the handicapped.

And one of his first topics of conversation will be the building's washrooms, and the fact that washroom doors open out, instead of in, to, he says, promote cleanliness.

Meijer's marketing strategy has gained recognition throughout the nation's retail industry and received a number of regional and national marketing awards. The strategy is simple — get the most goods to the most people at the lowest prices. A common strategy for most large retailers, but one which the Meijer family has developed into a science.

Meijer will be the first to tell shoppers not to visit his stores if they want well-organized shelves and catchy displays. He asks shoppers to compare prices around town, and says the store here will not rely solely on the Meijer reputation to lure buyers from other Traverse City stores.

Meijer is coy about making an estimate of the size of the chunk he expects the new store to carve out of the

Fred Meijer is coy when asked about sales projections during conversation about the Traverse City store and Meijer's market's operations. (Record-Eagle photos by Dann Persaky)

Traverse City retail market. He says he may have known the figure a year ago when the chain made its decision to locate here, but has forgotten it since.

Traverse City Meijer's store director Lloyd Whipple is equally as cagey. He says he wouldn't venture a guess on the store's first-year gross because of the unusual nature of the Traverse City retail market.

Meijer doesn't want to detract from the Traverse City market, he says, he wants to add to it. "I hope there is business enough for all of us. I think we will increase Traverse City's draw".

He says he "understands" that some Traverse City grocery store owners may be apprehensive about the Meijer's impact on the market. "I want the Traverse City trading center to be vibrant, and I think we will add to that."

At least one Traverse City grocery chain owner isn't apprehensive about Meijer's entrance into the market. Gerald Oleson, a 35-year friend of the Meijer's family, offered to sell Meijer land in Traverse City for a store three years ago. Oleson even offered to build the store for the Meijer's chain.

Although Meijer's cautions its

employes that costs increased drastically in 1976 while sales continued a normal rate of increase — thus generating less profit — the corporation did generate enough profit to open three new Thrifty Acres "hypermarkets" this year.

And Meijer says he doesn't know how much the three new stores will generate, or what the corporation's budget will be this year.

Members of the Meijer's board say the company's chief executive generally is oblivious to the everyday financial matters of the chain. He concentrates on the Meijer's "human image," focusing on shopper comforts and energy conservation.

Meijers is regarded as somewhat of a fanatic on cleanliness and energy conservation and the human side of the retail industry by his colleagues. Meijer's reputation doesn't bother him. He may even work to retain it.

It's not unusual for Meijer to eat his meals in one of the Thrifty Acres cafeterias. He breakfasted on sausage and eggs in the Meijer's cafeteria during the Traverse City store's grand opening Tuesday morning.

It's also not unusual for Meijer to be

greeted by salutations of "Hi Fred" from clerks or stockers when he walks employe by his first name. Generally, the salutation is returned with a friendly "How are you," or "Gentlemen."

Meijer said he doesn't believe in formal titles, and bases his prejudice on his European upbringing. Both his parents are from the Netherlands, and dislike any kind of class or racial prejudice, he says.

"I don't believe in 'Mr. This' or 'Mr. That'," Meijer said. "It's just another barrier."

Part of the Meijer's profit-generating philosophy is the motivation of its employes by good management-employe relations. Part of that motivation includes eliminating the less desirable jobs — and that's where the Meijer "hypermarket" concept was conceived.

Keeping a work force which is two-thirds the size of Traverse City's total population motivated isn't easy. Part of the key is Meijer's policy of hiring a large number — 75 percent — of part-time employes. Another key is a combination of fairly competitive wages and good benefits.

Top clerks at the Traverse City store receive $6 an hour, compared to approximately $6.40 paid at some downstate Meijer's stores. Part-timers receive pay equal to full-time employes, and also receive most benefits.

"We cannot pay this unless we step up production," Meijer said. That's where the "hypermarket" philosophy of bin and carton display — originally developed in Europe — comes in.

"Everything is on wheels, keep it rolling," that's the Meijer's key to low prices, Meijer said. "As little is double-handled as possible."

Meijer looked almost indigant as he walked through his Traverse City store before its opening Monday when he noticed that most of the cereal boxes were arranged with the labels showing.

"They pulled a fast one on us," Meijer said, describing store director Whipple's sprucing up of the store for the grand opening.

"They won't be that way for long."

The Meijer philosophy of shelf stacking — boxes upside down, merchandise often placed on beat-up carts, cans thrown in bins — is unusual from a man who is known" as a fanatic for cleanliness.

Meijer says it really isn't too surprising just a matter of finances. He says that shoppers would rather see a box upside down than pay an extra nickle for a box of well-displayed cereal.

But the floors of Meijer's store on U.S. 31 always will be spotless, the back rooms clean, the meat department almost sterile.

"No matter how low our prices are, people wouldn't shop here if it wasn't clean," Meijer said. "If I wouldn't buy my food here, I wouldn't expect anyone else to come here either."

"He concentrates on the company's 'human image,' focusing on shopper comforts and energy conservation," said a reporter in this 1978 profile

their homes, and they leave two or three times, and finally they turn to stand and fight and then we say, "You're savages. You just won't give us your home."

• There is more to life than making a fast buck. You think about that and the old Chevy slogan, "Getting there is half the fun." It is half wrong. I think it's all the fun. Getting there is all the fun, being there isn't any fun. We had just as much fun with one store as we do with our 20 some big stores and 40 little ones looking forward to the future.

*Fred's speeches can be surprising in their candor. Here he addresses a 1978
gathering of economics teachers in Grand Rapids*

SCARCITY

When my father first came over from the Netherlands he
talked about having to obtain hunting and fishing licenses
back home. "Oh," said the Americans, "We would never stand
for that here."

He talked about needing a permit to chop down a tree and
the Americans laughed. We are not laughing anymore. We are
slowly becoming just as densely populated as Europe has
been for some time. As there are more people in the world, we
must learn to use our resources more wisely--decide whether
we should use a piece of land for a store, a home, or a farm.

ENJOYING CHANGE

We are all going to have to learn to enjoy change. I run two
miles each morning in the hopes that I will live a good long
time and get to see more of what is going to happen. I think
we are living in a thrilling time.

At the company's first awards banquet, in 1951, Fred and the family honored five people. Twenty-five years later, Fred spoke to 1,000 associates

As an offshoot of his enthusiasm for skiing, Fred began installing his own bindings in his basement workshop

SUNDAY OPENINGS

What most people don't realize, when you start a business, you do things that nobody else wants to do. Way back when we first started in the grocery business we were open nights, Sundays and holidays. We were open when nobody else wanted to be open, and once we got rolling and got a good enough business, we didn't have to work Sundays and holidays. We closed the store. So we were closed for a lot of years. But we did start out that way.

Then, when we were in the department store business, I think, and Arlan's and K-Mart were open Sundays, we said, "Wow, if we're not open Sundays because we are in the supermarket business, we're not giving the same service that other people are giving and sooner or later we are going backwards."

You have several prime responsibilities to yourself, as far as I am concerned. You have the people that work with you and their careers. You have people who are with you their whole lives. We owe it to them to run a business that is going to be in business a year from now, five years from now, 10 years from now. We owe it to our creditors, to people who loan us the money, because we borrow more money than we are worth, by far, to pay our bills, and to run our business.

And then you still want the joy of running a business that is *in* business. So for example when K-Mart went into Holland, Michigan, we thought for sure they'd open Sundays, for they were open everyplace else. So we opened Sundays and all heck broke loose and they kept closed in Holland and Jenison even though they were open every place else, and that kind of left us high and dry. It was a tough time, but we weathered it. Basically, if you're right enough, even though you get a lot of criticism, sooner or later you do come through. But of course how do you know you're always right?

You do things that the competition doesn't want to do and then they hate your guts for doing it, but the customers come. And so that's why we opened Sundays. In Grand Rapids people said if your dad was alive, he wouldn't be open Sundays, but we got our start being open late nights and Sundays. I probably worked 40 to 50 hours a week in the store during

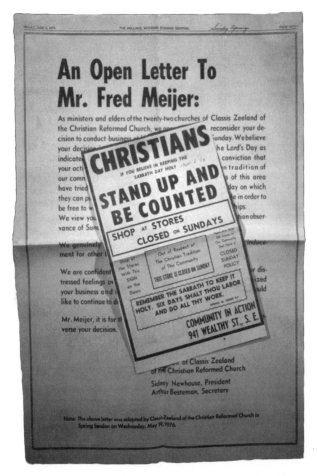

A decision to open Meijer stores on Sundays in Grand Rapids in 1969, and in Holland and Jenison in 1978, drew the wrath of some residents in the interest of serving others. Lost in the vitriol was an awareness that the little store in Greenville had often been open on Sundays to accommodate the needs of its customers

high school. I never went to one basketball game in high school or football game or anything. I mean I just came back from school and worked in the store and practiced violin a little bit and did some studying but basically I worked in the store.

FUTURE EXPANSION

We have surveyed most of Michigan and have the research completed and have concluded that the most logical places for expansion in Michigan would be the cities of Saginaw, Bay City, Midland, Mount Pleasant, Alma, Big Rapids, Cadillac, Adrian, St. Joe and Benton Harbor. With the possibilities of an energy crisis and the dependency of all of Michigan on the auto industry, we've been looking to see whether it's sound planning to do all our expansion in these areas. Or, should we look elsewhere? We have thought about the possibility of going over the border into South Bend and Fort Wayne, because these areas are as close to our headquarters in general, or as easy to get to in general, as Traverse City. Now we are researching Northern Indiana in a line from the south side of Fort Wayne to the south side of South Bend.

PROMOTING FROM WITHIN

I am obsessed with promoting from within. The guy from the outside, he will have his own philosophies. He may have a good track record, but what if his beliefs are counter to what we have evolved?

DIGNITY

Today we teach courses on management by objective and human dignity. I'm a firm believer that if we could treat people with proper dignity, management by objective falls into place. If we do a good job with management by objective, we'll automatically treat people with human dignity, because if you help people to achieve their goal, if a manager feels that it's his or her job to help the people working for him or her to be successful, then you're automatically practicing the best of human dignity. At the same time, that's management by objective. Basically, I think they are one and the same.

Delegate - Don't abdicate

CHAPTER 7

~

THE 80s

JUST ASK LENA
Once in a while I get into mischief with my conversations.

KNOWING NAMES
A lot of associates know me and I am embarrassed that I cannot call them by name. I am just not gifted with that good a memory.

SATISFACTION
I don't think I've given an order for 10 or 20 years. The only time I give an order is if I see an ice cream cone on the floor and somebody is liable to slip. But basically my fun is in watching people develop. If people do things that we never thought they could do, and they never thought they would do, we can build the company and at the same time give careers and income to people that they wouldn't have had—that's satisfying. Give people security they wouldn't have had, give young people coming out of high school the opportunity to work in a free-market enterprise that treats them with dignity so they say, "Hey, this is what business is all about. It's not about abusing people, it's not just about making money, it's about service and enjoying being part of the community." I enjoy being part of things, more than if I was retired and living in some remote spot. So I've chosen not to. We don't have two homes. We don't have a home on Mackinac Island or in Florida. I enjoy this more than golf, or I'd be playing golf.

RELIGION
My father had a great interest in religion. Entire cultures of the world are influenced by religion. If you can study all the religions in the world, there are wonderful things in all of them. I don't happen to believe that one is right and superior to the others, there is good in all of them. If you can bring out all of that it is just a wonderful education.

TOILET DOORS
Sanitation is important, and part of that is toilet doors opening out. We'll have to save that for an in-depth discussion about toilet doors.

An interest in others helps keep Fred a driving force in the company, c. 1983

PAST AND FUTURE (1982)

This is the most unsettled, uncharted time economically that we, as a company, have ever known. However, this is not the only time. I was 14 years old when we went into the grocery business in Greenville in 1934, and that was an unsettled time for my father.

Our problems today are ones we have not experienced before. One is the energy shortage.

Electronic shopping is another big question. I understand some retailers have made quite a commitment to this project, and have an ideal vehicle if they should develop their catalogs for video use. We do not have that. For us, it would be a complete change of direction if we were to go to catalog shopping.

Extraordinary interest rates certainly add to the present dilemma. I do not know whether they will be down or up again. Some economists are predicting that interest rates could go as low as 8 or 9 percent, while others are predicting rates as high as 20 or 30 percent. Knowledgeable judgment about where the economy is going cannot be made when economists cannot agree.

DIVERSIFICATION & EXPANSION

We have done extensive research on how to best expand. We stuck our toes in the water with other ventures. With all these toes stuck in the water, we have to make something work.

The first two Meijer Square stores did not show heavy start-up losses like a Thrifty Acres does, so we proceeded with the Twin Fair purchase. This was done after establishing that we should go only where we could transport merchandise from the Grand Rapids and Lansing distribution centers.

The decision to purchase Twin Fair was based on distribution requirements as well as on the distance for buyers, specialists and other managers to travel. We took one trip to Florida and it was a long day; long hours in a plane are not practical for us. A Meijer operation in Florida or Oklahoma would have to be completely on its own.

We decided that 300 miles is the maximum distance we can

The company marked its 50th anniversary in 1984 with Lena and Fred help-ing bury a time capsule near the entrance of the Fred Meijer Building

expand and still use our present shipping base. We could not go 300 miles north or we would be in Canada; west, and we would have to cross Lake Michigan; east, and we are in Canada again.

Our decision was to go south through Ohio and Indiana. We can travel to Cincinnati in an hour by airplane. However, when we chose this area, we limited ourselves to the industri-al Midwest, which is having the worst economic problems in the country.

MAKE THE JOB AS GOOD AS YOU ARE

I remember this dissatisfied grocer. I think he got kicked out of the University of Michigan, but he always felt he was too good for the grocery business. He felt he should be a doctor in his own mind, when, in reality, he probably wasn't good enough for the business. That being the case, the business succeeded only to a point and then died. Probably he went through his whole life thinking that he was miscast in the grocery job. Instead of thinking, "I'm going to make this job as good as I am," in his own mind he thought the job wasn't as good as he was, was below his dignity. He always had that condescending air about him which even infected new young people who would come to work for him.

HAVING FUN

Outside of making a basic living, if they can make it someplace else, they should not be in our business unless they can have fun in it.

MY WARDROBE

See this [a blue polyester blazer]? I paid $20 for it at a clearance sale in one of our stores.

MAKING MONEY

We do not make a heck of a lot of money, and it does not matter. The public companies have to perform and pay dividends; if we make a little over one percent in profit, we are happy.

NEVER FORGET

The bitter taste of poor quality remains long after the sweet taste of a low price.

LONG-TIME BOAST

I'm the most in-debt person in the state of Michigan.

We believe in enlightened selfishness

The once-shy boy from Greenville thrives on conversation

I gave a talk at a grade School in G.R.
    & received the following letter.

"Thank you for taking the time to
    visit Sibley School. I learned nothing
    but it was a good speech"
                    Sincerely
                        Amanda Kishman

CARL SANDBURG

Someone, I think it was my sister, gave me a set of Carl Sandburg's records, "The People, Yes." And they talk about pride and prejudice and proverbs and why do the kids put beans in their ears when you tell the kids not to put beans in their ears and why do we treat and call the Chinese yellow dogs when they were good enough to build our railroads? We didn't need them after they built our railroads to the west and then we called them yellow dogs. A lot of prejudice proverbs made a big impression on me, and I've used those proverbs and Carl Sandburg's quotations almost all my life.

I guess between my father's racial attitudes and my mother's racial attitudes and the teacher and Carl Sandburg and a little thinking of my own, it's amazing how you develop your racial feelings, and from your feelings come your actions. It certainly affected me in my racial attitudes and and my religious attitudes all my life.

EARNING YOUR BUSINESS

We know we have to earn our business. After we are here five to 10 years we hope our customers will say they cannot get along without Meijer.

FEEL FOR PEOPLE

My dad always had a real feel for people and he expressed it in many ways. I am sure that had an influence on me. My mother did also. Her family was involved in political activities in the Netherlands.

DIGNITY IN WORK

My dad felt there was dignity in work, that anyone who worked deserved complete respect. For example: some of his best friends were people that average society might call kind of dull or not very prosperous. But he felt that if a man worked with his hands, or worked in a factory or worked on a farm, or if you were a banker or a business person, any person who worked for a living was worthwhile. He respected education, but he would not be any more enamored if someone had a doctor's degree than if he spent the 20 years cleaning toilets in a Thrifty Acres.

Fred with Judge Benjamin Gibson, c. 1985

WOMEN IN THE WORKFORCE

I was constantly exposed to an atmosphere that touched on dignity for all races, dignity for poor people and dignity for handicapped people. The same thing is true for women. My sister ran the first store for the first year and my wife worked in the store for 10 years. My mother worked on the family farm for years, and later spent many years working in the store. My dad just felt that anyone could do most anything. The question of whether women should have a certain job did not really cross our minds. Around 1948, we had our first cashier trainer, who was a woman. We also had a female office manager and the first supervisor of our data processing department was a woman.

ORIGINS OF THE SUPERCENTER

We opened the first Thrifty acres in 1962. But earlier than that, we created a department within the supermarket that was rather large for a supermarket. It had some children's wear, and it had health and beauty care items, and it had some toys, and those sort of things. That gave us a feel, a little bit of a head start.

WHY WE NEED TO GROW

If you lose a little hair every day or a little skin every day, or a piece of a fingernail, and if that fingernail and that hair and that skin were not growing, you would soon be a hairless, skinless, fingernailless person. Companies and stores are like that. Some locations will become obsolete. Some different factors would happen in the markets and if you do not grow some to replace that hair, you will end up bald. So we think you have to grow some to be a sound company. Now how fast you grow, that is a matter of debate.

CONFIDENCE IN PEOPLE

You have to have confidence in people. Confidence in their ability, confidence in their integrity. You have to have a feeling of joy when they progress and do things that you like to do and do them better than maybe you could do.

I think one of the biggest problems of parents is sometimes they are jealous of their children's youth, and they can never believe that that child will grow up, no matter how old the child is. If a child wants to go to a dance or a ballgame, they should never tell their child, "You cannot go because I am your parent and I say you can't." That is not a good enough reason. The same thing is true in business.

WELCOMING CHANGE

The very things we fear usually end up making us better merchants providing better quality for the customer.

Teamwork is paramount in Fred's approach to life. Above, Saginaw associates in front of their store, 1982. Below, Fred and part of the original team at the Cascade store in Grand Rapids, 1984

VISITING STORES

I like to learn. I mean, I do not come to a store to pick up the paper in the parking lot, but if I am on the parking lot, I pick up the paper. I do not come to shove the carts in, although if I come in, I bring in a couple of carts. I do not come in to supervise the store. If I happen to see something that I think should be done, I think it is my job to mention it, not to go back and end up with "Fred saw it; and why didn't he say something while he was here?"

If I see something wrong in the store, it is my job to discuss it, but I am not looking for it. I am looking to learn what is going on. It keeps me from getting in the proverbial ivory tower, so that I can still understand what's going on.

WHO WE WORK WITH

We recently spent more than $200,000 to settle a lawsuit with an employee we fired for making disparaging remarks against and refusing to work with a black manager. It cost us a lot of money, but there was no way I wanted someone like that working in our store.

BEFORE THE STORE

My dad was a barber for 27 years and he wanted to teach me to be a barber and work my way through college.

Well, I never went to college, but I think I might have been a school teacher or principal or maybe even a superintendent.

IF MY DAD WERE ALIVE

What would my dad think of the business today? He would laugh and enjoy every minute of it. He would be as flabbergasted and as surprised as I am.

We wouldn't have this company if I couldn't have worked with my dad

Grand Rapids artist Paul Collins created this mural in 1985 to hang in the Fred Meijer Building. Portrayed along with the family are (upper right) Earl Holton and Harvey Lemmen, as well as Charles Sims, one of the original Thrift Market's then-surviving customers, and Dennis Guernsey (in cap), long-time Meijer associate who helped build and renovate many of the company's early stores

not grown up until you can accept your parents with their faults

IF OTHERS AGREE

For years now, if Harvey Lemmen and Earl Holton agreed, I have not reversed them once. Now, if our two sons and the president [Holton] agree, I tell them ahead of time, "I will not reverse you."

Usually, on a big deal, we come to a consensus.

UNION, 1980

Let me tell you what we did. We had very tough union problems three years ago. The people were split between nonunion, independent union--which was in our stores since 1951--and the retail clerks UFCW, who had taken over the independent union's officership. There were three different factions.

We had the lawyers in, we had the key people in, and we had all three of our sons in on every deliberation that they could be part of, and we had a vote.

BUYING TWIN FAIR

Three of our key people were not there that day. Fifteen were there, and the vote to buy these stores was five for and 10 against. The five of us won. But they had their vote, you know. Now just because you involve everybody, you still cannot abdicate your responsibility for your position. The reason we bought these stores is because conditions have changed some. Mortgages are higher. Building costs are higher and I think we're going to have to recycle old buildings more than we used to. Now, the 10 people who voted against it--some of them feel that we can go on like we always did. Maybe we can, maybe we can't. And so we did have a vote, and I was able to use that in the negotiations in New York and tell them two-thirds of our people that we polled don't want it.

Don't give blame for bad Ideas
Give Credit for Good Ideas

Fred, Harvey, Earl, 1982

ADVENTURE

I've had a lot of experiences. We're going to go bike riding for a week in western Canada in September. I went bike riding in the Netherlands, and we walked in New Zealand on the Milford Track, and we rode horses in the desert. You've got to find time for something different along with business. You can have a lot of fun in business. Nobody has more fun than I do. But there have to be other things so that you don't go stale doing nothing but business. Because the world isn't all business, the world is everything combined.

IT'S ALWAYS BEEN FUN

I remember Sam Cook, an old patriarch of the supermarket industry. He said, and I hope I'm quoting him correctly, he once said, "You work to get there and when you is there, where are you?"

MY ROLE

I have delegated everything possible. It is ego deflating, because when you ask people to do a job, they cannot keep you involved and informed every step of the way. You put yourself on the outside somewhat and do not always know what is going on.

REASONS FOR SHOPPING WITH US

The word must have gone out that Meijer had good prices and was a good place to shop and was probably equal to the best, but that is only part of it. You see, if you are equal to the best, as far as low prices are concerned, people will want to trade with you for reasons other than price. Customers have both a monetary and emotional reason for trading with a store. The welfare administrator of Montcalm County could not understand how we got 60 percent of all the welfare business in the county. We did the things we thought were right, and it worked out. We treated poor people with dignity.

A Meijer bag goes along as Fred traces the Silk Road route of Marco Polo on a Smithsonian Institution trip across Asia in 1988

FAMILY BUSINESS

We almost went broke a few times, and we were broke to start but never bankrupt. Sometimes you're worse than that, but nobody wants to foreclose on you. I was a party to all the problems as far as knowing what went on in the family business, as a small child and on up. When somebody was buying a nickel Coke after school back in my high school days, I would not think of spending a nickel for Coke because a nickel was a lot of money. As our family grew, we got ourselves in a few financial jams.

Then when we've had opportunities to sell out from time to time, I called the family together--I don't do that any more because our company can't be bought--but I called them together and said, "We have this opportunity," and to a person, whether it be my wife or my children--our children, my wife had something to do with it, too--anyway, they said no.

The youngest one said, "I can't see myself in the business. But then when we talked about selling, he said it wouldn't be the same. I said, "Sure it wouldn't be the same. Somebody else would own it." So we've had these family consultations. Right now all three of our sons are on the board of directors. Doug and Hank are co-chairmen. Doug has been chairing our weekly management committee meetings, and Hank has been chairing the board meetings. I want them as involved as they want to be or as disinvolved as they want to be. Looking forward to the future, if it can't be that same fun for the people coming in as members of your family, they shouldn't be in.

There's one thing my dad said when he visited another guy. The fellow that was mad because his son wouldn't come into the business, and this was a family business and so forth. My dad says, "Did you go home and tell your son all the problems of the business and never the good side?"

And he says, "Henry, maybe you're right." As our family is growing up, we have to tell them, there's something good. It isn't just competition that's bad and unions that are problems, and the newspaper raised the rates, and inflation is here, and the government is going to pot.

Communicating, 1982

Maybe we should say, "My gosh, we never thought we would have it so good. This is a good business we're in, and we're enjoying it," and so sprinkle in the joy along with problems. I've tried to do that. I don't know if I've been successful. I don't think anybody is successful till after you're dead, and they look back and see how you messed things up or you did not.

RUNNING SCARED

I have been scared ever since we have been in the grocery business. I live scared. We have survived by evolution in the development of our business, but I want our people to run scared to do their darndest to compete.

BALANCE IN A FAMILY BUSINESS

I think the people who are operating the business should have more to say about the business than the people who are not in the business, and yet the people who are not in the business should be able to share in whatever progress it makes financially. The people on the inside will always get more perks just being on the inside in the way of wages and other benefits, in addition to whatever the stock ownership is worth. So you've got to be sure that you're fair with the outsiders. But if they've chosen to be outsiders, I think the insiders should run the company.

OUR KIDS

Well, of course, they grew up in it. I told them they could have anything money could buy as long as they earned it, and the one thing nice about a family business is that you can provide jobs for your own kids as they're growing up. I mean, there are millions of young people in the United States who can't find anything to do for pin money and have to steal it or something else, and that's where a family company has a definite advantage in the early years. Hank started working in the stores at 11 or 12 when he had to fold his apron over double. People were very nice to him. They looked down on him, kind or patted him on the head. As he grew older he says, "You know, I missed something when I grew taller and they treated me like another clerk."

I had the fortunate experience of working with my father for about 35 or 40 years. We had a relationship that was closer than--well, as close as is possible. It's not possible for me to have this same close relationship with our three sons. There are three of them instead of one. Our business has grown. I started nailing wooden lath on the first store before we opened it. I was 14 years old. I was so fortunate that my father never treated me like a little kid.

Doug, Fred, Hank, Earl, 1988

SURVIVAL

If we have a business that can only survive if the family members come in, if the life or death of the business depends on whether or not they come in, I don't think that's fair to the company. And it's not fair to the family.

OUR VISION

We did not want to run a 'hoity-toity' store, but to cater to the masses. We never tried to run a carriage trade operation.

A BETTER IDEA

You try to let the employees have their way as much as possible. I will win more by having their best ideas than by forcing mine down their throats.

The most prominent breach of the Berlin Wall, as captured in this memorable Time magazine photograph from 1989, came just to the left of where someone had written the name Meijer. Fred obtained that section of the wall, which now resides inside the VanAndel Museum Center in Grand Rapids, as well as two others for display in the Grand Rapids area. The section at left stands in front of the Gerald R. Ford Museum

CHAPTER 8
~
THE 90s

THE IMPACT WE HAVE

Wherever we establish a store, we want people to think that Meijer did something to improve a town and the town is better off because we came.

SELF-MADE?

None of us is self-made. I was sensitized by my dad.

SATISFACTION

I get my biggest satisfaction from being part of something for progress.

NIET IK, NIET JIJ, MAAR WIJ

I hope I don't goof it all up. It says, "Not I, not you, but we." Management in the stores, team leaders in the stores, people in the stores. We all need each other. "It's not I, it's not you, it's we." I think it was one of my dad's favorite sayings, and its become one of my favorite sayings, Niet ik.

A SENSE OF COMMUNITY

I have a lot of good feeling from the Urban League days. I was the first to propose a black man, Paul Phillips, to come into Grand Rapids Rotary. Nobody opposed it, but nobody proposed it. When I proposed it, of course, Judge Letts was asked to be in the Lions Club, and it just kind of broke down the barriers that were maybe not quite there, but nobody addressed them. Then I worked seven years to bring women into Rotary. Social organizations are one thing, some people said, but Rotary is for businessmen to meet businessmen, and I couldn't sell it for seven years. But finally when some court case came down, women were accepted, and I sponsored one of the first two women in the Grand Rapids Rotary. So I feel good about that.

I feel good about our participation in the public broadcast field [at Grand Valley State University's Meijer Public Broadcast Center], because it does provide alternative programming. There are a lot of arguments about the quality of TV and so forth, but public broadcasting is in a little different posture; they have a different flavor to their programs.

Fred dances with Thrifty. Below, he strolls through the Meijer store in Westland, Michigan with actor James Whitmore, who served as the company's spokesman in a memorable series of television commercials describing "the store built on common sense"

YOU PAY TO GO TO COLLEGE

I was very fortunate that my dad treated me objectively. He never seemed to treat me like a little kid. He treated me like a person. Never did he ever bawl me out in public--or in private hardly, that I can recall. If we made a mistake, he would say, "You have to pay to go to college," meaning, you don't learn without mistakes, and mistakes are going to cost you something.

I made a mistake once on a butter advertisement in the paper, and I wanted to run a correction. I think I ran it 10 cents a pound below cost or something, and he said, "Don't do that. Let it go out. Let the people feel that we have a real bargain. Don't tell them you made a mistake, just make the best of it."

RESPECT & DIGNITY

If I respect his dignity, he will be a better man and feel better in his job and do a better job. We get a better job done for the money and if we're paying him, we like to get everything out of him we can. So, if a little soft soap does it, I'm working on it.

We don't have an unimportant job in our company. Who do we treat as the most important person in most organizations? The porter that cleans the toilet? You know, "any stupid fool can clean a toilet," yet every one of us here uses it and who of us wants to clean it? Therefore, if we've got a guy cleaning the toilets and doing a good job, it's bad enough maybe we pay him the lowest pay for cleaning the toilets, but then we look down on him besides? If we could look at him as an important person who cleans the toilet, and how he's a valuable part of our sanitation program, he will be proud to do his job of cleaning toilets right. This is what I'm talking about when I say we have a horizontal organizational chart. Very few people ever see this chart, but we want to be sure he feels that he is an important individual in our company. If we can make him feel important and then make him feel the job is important, then we're halfway towards getting the courtesy that we want and the job done that we want.

Fred serves turkey to Michigan National Guard troops in Greenville on the eve of their departure for Operation Desert Storm, November 19, 1990

CRITICIZE IN PRIVATE

You should never change a person's responsibilities without letting them know. Everyone should have only one boss, and if you're going to criticize somebody, criticize them in private. Compliment them in public.

Every time you criticize someone in public, their defenses go up and they don't hear what you're talking about anyway. So, we try to do some of those things to have our employees feel a sense of worth. If we treat them with value, then in turn they will treat us and the customers and the job with value. No one person in our company is any more important than another.

HONESTY IS THE BEST POLICY

I remember very distinctly one time our driver came in from Columbian Storage Warehouse with the truck, and I think he'd gotten 10 cases of merchandise which they forgot to bill us for. He came to me, and he said, "You know, many a time we've waited and many a time we've claimed things that they should have given us credit for, and they haven't, so by golly, this time we got some of our money back because they gave us 10 cases and didn't charge for it."

I can remember saying,"What would we have done if they had shorted us 10 cases?"

He said, "Well, we'd have hollered about it."

I said, "Then I think we should tell them that we got 10 cases that we didn't get billed for."

I have a feeling he was helping me justify it, and I also had a feeling that he felt good about the fact that we reported it back to them, but he was just letting me make the decision in the way he told me about the 10 cases.

Later on, at Grand Rapids Wholesaler [now Spartan Stores], two times we were underbilled. Once for $10,000, and another time for $9,000. Both times they never would have caught their mistake, and they said to me, after we told them about it, "It sure is funny nobody else had this problem." Well, I couldn't help but think nobody else probably had the problem because if they got underbilled, they didn't tell them about it. We did tell them about it in both instances, but the first time was $10,000 and that was a fortune to us in those days, and I could easily see where it could be tempting not to report it. Yet when we did, we felt better about it.

ADVERTISING

Advertising sums up a lot of your business philosophy, and on top of the dignity and on top of the customer relations, you aim for quality and honesty.

Below, Fred and sons Mark (left), Doug and Hank with an Isetta at the 1992 opening of the first SourceClub membership warehouse, in Okemos, Michigan, echoing the photo (left) of Fred and Hendrik nearly four decades earlier

FREDERIK MEIJER GARDENS

I hope the Frederik Meijer Gardens will do many things. One is to expose young people to art, to sculpture. My grandmother Meijer, my dad's mother, always said, "The eye wants something, too." There has to be more to life than getting up in the morning and going to bed at night, working and eating. This is where symphonies come in, and civic theater and plays and dance, where opera comes in. I guess what makes me so excited about the Botanic Garden is we are exposing people to nature. When I was young we used to have horses, we had the farm, we lived in a small town, we were close to the country, and even people in Grand Rapids were close to the country. Now what was country is all housing developments. People need a place to walk with nature, a place to learn about ecology.

Peter Wege and I spoke on the first Earth Day, about 22 or 23 years ago, at what is now the Welsh Auditorium in the Civic Center in Grand Rapids, and we've always been interested in recycling and baling, in preserving the air, the water and the land. We've always tried to be part of that, and this just all fits in. Maybe we can teach people to enjoy preserving the air, water and land, learn about it, why they should do it, why it's for all of our own good. I'm very serious about the educational aspects.

And there is a third dimension: one of the sculptures we're having created shows 11 children playing together, including one Asian, one Native American Indian, one Hispanic, one Caucasian, one African, one with Down Syndrome, one with leg braces. In this world we've got to learn to get along with all races, all nationalities, all religions--to understand physical and mental differences among us — and we've got to learn to appreciate our differences and enjoy people who are different, rather than fear people who are different. Most of our prejudices are based on fear, and fear is based on not knowing, on ignorance. I don't mean ignorance in that a person is ignorant, but that he is ignorant of the joy of knowing other cultures, other races. This is why I enjoy working yet, at 74 years old, because I meet people, I get into things, I get into controversies I wouldn't know about if I were playing golf in Florida.

FREDERIK MEIJER
GARDENS

Michigan Botanic Garden & Meijer Sculpture Park

*Fred and Marshall Fredericks' bronze "Bear with Boy" on the bank of the
Grand River in downtown Grand Rapids, 1994. This sculpture and others
from the collection of the Frederik Meijer Gardens were placed temporarily
in and along the river for the city's Celebration on the Grand*

I wish I was 25 again + Could
live another 50 -to - 100 years.

Fred and Peter Wege, noted philanthropist and president of the Michigan Botanic Garden Foundation, discuss plans for the Frederik Meijer Gardens while visiting the site in 1993

Fred, Lena and grandchildren at home, 1994

HEALTH

I've been very lucky. I talked to a young man at the Alpine Avenue store who is 16 years old and smokes. He has smoked for seven years, since he was nine. He's now pushing in carts for us and picking up paper in the lot and bagging—and spending $20 a week for cigarettes. That makes me feel bad, because all the people of my high school class who smoked and drank are either almost incapacitated or dead, with very few exceptions. I'm talking mostly about the males. I'm so lucky that I didn't smoke. It isn't a moral thing with me, it's just an accident, and I sure am pleased.

To go walking in the woods is one thing I like about the Botanical Gardens—walking is such wonderful exercise. I don't do much of it, I don't do enough of it, but I've done it for many years. If I wasn't a little too heavy I'd be doing things more right. My mother was a vegetarian. I read in a Harvard health book last night that the closer we can come to being vegetarians, the better. We've got to lay off the fats.

*Fred is frequently airborne,
keeping in touch with Meijer people
and plans in a five-state area*

Fred rarely misses a grand opening, including this one in Fort Wayne, Indiana in 1994 which helped mark the debut of a new generation of Meijer stores

Don Magoon (left), Johanna Magoon, Lena and Fred in Ypsilanti, Michigan, 1994

LOOK, MA--NO HANDS

I used to ride with no hands down Main Street. I love to ride a bike no hands. About three years ago I rode a bike one night to see how far I could go. I rode it nine miles, with no hands, around the cemetery. On level ground you have to be leaning in a certain way. Actually, you've got to be leaning out and in at the same time to ride a bike no hands when you go around a corner. You find out you've got to stick your rump in one direction and lean in the other to make the bike go where you want it to go.

Almost never say never

The original Thrifty Acres, Store #11, marks the company's 60th anniversary in 1994 with a new troop of pony riders (below) in a familiar pose. Joining Fred and Lena in the front row are Harold Hans (second from left) and Dave Plasman. At rear, from left, are Hank Meijer, Fred Welling, Bill Smith and Dick Gilpin

THE DIGNITY OF WHAT WE DO

If you can treat people like they want to be treated, if you can treat people like they are needed, if you can recognize people as human beings—like you want to be recognized—and if you can say how as a team leader or manager you can help people to succeed, you don't need to show people how smart you are, you need to show people how smart they can be.

If you have an area of responsibility you'll look plenty fine because they are helping you to succeed. You can't do it alone. You need people.

Everybody in some part of our organization is smarter than I am, in some area of expertise, be it in knowing how to cut meat, or to process produce, or whatever. Everybody in information systems, in warehousing, in driving a hi-lo—everybody knows something I don't know. If we can help those people to succeed without me having to know all those things, it makes a winning combination.

We've got to run the company in such a way that we stay in business. You can be idealistic, but if you don't stay in business, you can't deliver on idealism. So you have to be pragmatic and idealistic at the same time. That means being practical.

I hope we can continue with our philosophies and not have to lose them or abandon them, and at the same time run a company that people can be pleased to work with, proud to work with—one that is looked upon as an asset to the community. If it is win-win all-round, then I think we are on the road to the right things. So many people lose this when they sell out or go public, or when they get into a financial crisis. And every time we go into a financial crisis we rely on it, rather than losing it.

I think you can keep the core values best by going back to the well, and the well is the people working in the company. If you go back to them and say. "What do you think we need to do? Where do you think we're wrong? Where do you think we're right? What needs to be preserved? What needs to be

In rare black tie, c. 1994

thrown out? What needs to be altered?"

The knowledge is with the people who are in the company. The knowledge isn't with management alone, although it has a lot of knowledge. The knowledge isn't with anyone alone, we all need management, need team leaders. The knowledge of the total group — if you can bring that out you'll have a winning combination to adapt to the future.

No one of us knows what the future holds, but that is what is so exciting. That is why, even though I know I won't, I want to live to be 100 years old.

Still blazing trails!